Glencoe Language Arts

Vocabulary Power

Grade 6

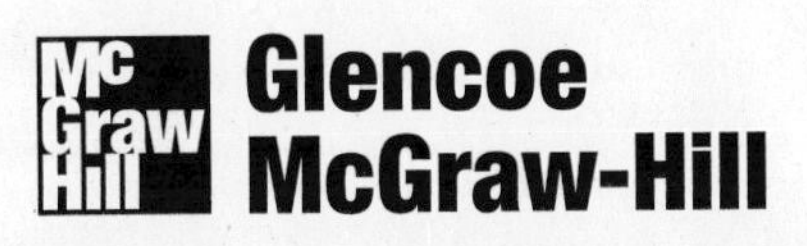

New York, New York Columbus, Ohio Woodland Hills, California Peoria, Illinois

To the Teacher

Vocabulary Power is a workbook that offers exercises, skills practice, reviews, and tests to expand student word power and to develop a deeper understanding of language. The vocabulary is selected from a variety of sources, including standardized tests, the *Living Word Vocabulary,* and *Roget's Thesaurus.* Designed to build communication power, *Vocabulary Power* enables students to grow as thinkers, readers, speakers, and writers.

Glencoe/McGraw-Hill

A Division of The **McGraw-Hill** *Companies*

Send all inquiries to:
Glencoe/McGraw-Hill
8787 Orion Place
Columbus, Ohio 43240

ISBN 0-02-818252-9

Printed in the United States of America

3 4 5 6 7 8 9 10 108 04 03 02 01

CONTENTS

Contents

Name ____________________ Date ____________ Class ____________

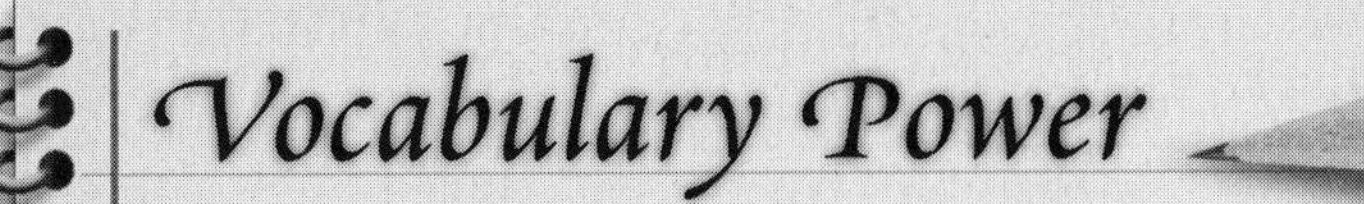

Lesson 1 Using Context Clues

Sometimes, we face new situations away from the comfort of our homes and families. Have you ever had to face an uncomfortable situation, wishing it were over before it started? Maybe your family moved, and you had to go to a new school where you didn't know anyone. Or perhaps you had to go to the dentist to get a filling for the first time. The words in the following list have to do with the feelings that you might have or actions you might take as you experience a new or uncomfortable situation.

Word List

alarm	**cope**	**mortified**	**resent**
anticipation	**defiance**	**pang**	**unique**
bewilderment	**hostile**		

EXERCISE A Context Clues

Fill in the blanks below with words from the list that best fit. Double-check your answers by looking up the meanings of these words in a dictionary.

1. The purple mouse with orange polka dots is definitely a(n) ____________ toy.
2. I looked on in ____________, hoping to see the new toy.
3. Trisha didn't like the ____________ looks Lucy was giving her.
4. The fire ____________ went off because I burned the bacon.
5. Sally began to ____________ the restrictions of her hospital stay.
6. We looked on in ____________ as the car salesman yelled at the car he was trying to sell.
7. How can we ____________ with students who won't sit still in class?
8. I respect the ____________ of Americans in the Revolutionary War.
9. He felt a ____________ for not taking Janet to the park.
10. The monk ____________ himself by penance and fasting.

EXERCISE B Usage

If the boldfaced word is used correctly in the sentence, write *correct* above it. If not, draw a line through the word and write the correct vocabulary word above it.

1. The scientist was excited when he discovered a **hostile** kind of rock.

2. With the bases loaded, the fans waited with great **anticipation** as their team's best batter stepped up to the plate.

3. He could tell from the **mortified** faces in the crowd that he was unwelcome.

4. The girls **resent** their classmates for telling on them.

5. The teacher realized that the students did not understand the question when she saw the look of **defiance** in their eyes.

EXERCISE C Multiple-Meaning Words

Several of the words in the list have more than one meaning. Fill in the word that best completes each sentence below. In the space provided to the left, write in the number of the definition that helped you make your choice.

hostile *adj.* **1.** of or having to do with an enemy **2.** unfriendly, opposed. *n.* **3.** an enemy; a hostile person
pang *n.* **1.** a sudden, short, piercing pain **2.** a sharp, sudden feeling
anticipation *n.* **1** act of looking forward to; expectation **2.** a prior action that takes into account a later action
alarm: *n.* **1.** a call to arms **2.** a signal **3.** sudden, sharp apprehension resulting from the perception of imminent danger

______ 1. The soldiers crouched silently in the bushes, watching in ______________ as the enemy troops marched by.

______ 2. In ______________ of the governor's overnight visit, city officials booked a suite of rooms in their city's finest hotel.

______ 3. The villagers could tell from the pilot's uniform and speech that he was a(n) ______________ and unwelcome visitor.

______ 4. The ______________ went off as soon as the driver opened his door.

______ 5. The man felt a(n) ______________ of regret as he left his homeland.

EXERCISE D Usage

On a separate sheet of paper, write sentences in which you use each of the words in the list correctly. The sentences should show that you understand the word meanings.

Name ______________________ Date ______________ Class ______________

Vocabulary Power

Lesson 2 The Prefixes *em-* and *en-*

A prefix is added to the beginning of a root or a base word to change its meaning. The prefixes *em-* and *en-* mean "in" or "into."

Word List

embroider	employ	endeavor	engaging
emphasize	enable	endorse	envelop
emphatic	encounter		

EXERCISE A Synonyms

Synonyms are words with similar meanings. Each boldfaced vocabulary word is paired with a synonym whose meaning you probably know. Think of other words related to the meaning of the synonym and write your ideas on the line provided. Then, look up the vocabulary word in a dictionary and write its meaning.

1. **embroider** : sew ______________________

   Dictionary definition ______________________

2. **emphasize** : stress ______________________

   Dictionary definition ______________________

3. **emphatic** : forceful ______________________

   Dictionary definition ______________________

4. **employ** : hire ______________________

   Dictionary definition ______________________

5. **enable** : allow ______________________

   Dictionary definition ______________________

6. **encounter** : meet ______________________

   Dictionary definition ______________________

7. **endeavor** : try ______________________

   Dictionary definition ______________________

8. **endorse** : support ______________________

   Dictionary definition ______________________

Vocabulary Power continued

9. **engaging** : charming ______________________

   Dictionary definition ______________________

10. **envelop** : surround ______________________

   Dictionary definition ______________________

EXERCISE B Multiple-Meaning Words

Several of the words in the list have more than one meaning. Fill in the word that best completes each sentence. In the space to the left, write in the number of the definition that helped you make your choice.

embroider *v.* **1.** to ornament a piece of material with stitches that create a raised design or pattern **2.** to make an ornament, pattern, or other design on cloth, leather, or other material with needlework **3.** to exaggerate; to add untrue details to
employ *v.* **1.** to provide with work and pay wages **2.** to use; make use of (someone or something) **3.** to occupy; to engage the attention of
endorse *v.* **1.** to sign one's name on the back of (a check or other document) to indicate its transfer or to assure that it is paid **2.** to express public support or approval of

_______ **1.** The Fraternal Order of Police decided not to ______________ any of the candidates for mayor in the upcoming election.

_______ **2.** As the company expanded, the owner decided to ______________ more people.

_______ **3.** Bricklayers ______________ a variety of different tools to build a chimney.

_______ **4.** Sometimes, people ______________ stories to make them sound more interesting to listeners.

_______ **5.** Bank tellers watch people ______________ their paychecks every day.

EXERCISE C Usage

On a separate sheet of paper, write a letter to a friend in which you use each of the words in the word list correctly. Your letter should show that you understand the meaning of each vocabulary word.

Name ______________________ Date ______________ Class ________

Vocabulary Power

Lesson 3 Using Synonyms

Home means different things to different people. It may mean the community we live in, our house or apartment, or anywhere we feel at home. The following words have to do with the place we call home.

Word List

abide	**edifice**	**reliance**	**sentiment**
communal	**kindred**	**resident**	**vicinity**
dwell	**nurture**		

EXERCISE A Synonyms

Each boldfaced vocabulary word is paired with a synonym whose meaning you probably know. Think of other words related to the meaning of the synonym and write them on the line provided. Then, look up the vocabulary word in a dictionary and write its meaning.

1. **abide** : tolerate ______________________

   Dictionary definition ______________________

2. **communal** : public ______________________

   Dictionary definition ______________________

3. **dwell** : live ______________________

   Dictionary definition ______________________

4. **edifice** : building ______________________

   Dictionary definition ______________________

5. **kindred** : family ______________________

   Dictionary definition ______________________

6. **nurture** : foster ______________________

   Dictionary definition ______________________

7. **reliance** : dependence ______________________

   Dictionary definition ______________________

8. **resident** : occupant ______________________

   Dictionary definition ______________________

9. **sentiment** : feeling ______________________

   Dictionary definition ______________________

10. **vicinity** : neighborhood ______________________

   Dictionary definition ______________________

EXERCISE B Antonyms

Write the vocabulary word that is most nearly *opposite* in meaning.

1. unrelated ______________
2. independence ______________
3. private ______________
4. neglect ______________

EXERCISE C Etymology

Latin is the origin of some words on the vocabulary list. For each Latin word given below, the definition has been provided. Write the vocabulary word that comes from the Latin root. Then, add another word that might be related to the same root. Check your word choices in the dictionary.

1. *residere:* to sit back, remain ______________
2. *communis:* common ______________
3. *vicinis:* neighborhood ______________
4. *nutrire:* to suckle, nourish ______________
5. *sentir:* to perceive, to feel ______________
6. *religare:* to tie back ______________
7. *aedificare:* to make a dwelling ______________

EXERCISE D Word Illustrations

Think about how the vocabulary words in this lesson relate to your idea of home. On a separate sheet of paper, draw a picture that illustrates the meaning of one or two of the words. Then, write a caption for your drawing, using the words you chose.

Name ______________________ Date ______________ Class ______________

Vocabulary Power

Lesson 4 Using Reference Skills

Using a Thesaurus

Have you ever struggled to think of just the right word but couldn't find it in a dictionary? A thesaurus could help you. A thesaurus, which looks like a dictionary and contains lists of words like a dictionary, contains a different kind of information. Whereas a dictionary gives definitions, a thesaurus provides synonyms, or words with similar meanings, and sometimes supplies antonyms, or words with opposite meanings.

A thesaurus may list words in alphabetical order, just like a dictionary, or list words by category and provide an alphabetical index at the back. Below is a sample thesaurus entry.

> **sincere** *adj.* candid, open, plain, honest, conscientious, scrupulous, honorable; **Antonym:** insincere, dishonest

EXERCISE A

The word *sincere* is used in each sentence. Using the sample thesaurus entry above, replace *sincere* with a synonym that fits better. For each replacement, write a sentence explaining your choice.

1. She answered in **sincere**, simple sentences. ______________________
2. Mary gave **sincere,** forthright testimony in court. ______________________
3. The **sincere** talk show host always told her guests exactly how she felt. ______________
4. Acknowledging defeat was the **sincere** thing to do. ______________________

EXERCISE B

List five words or phrases that are synonyms of the word *mighty*. Use a thesaurus.

1. ______________________
2. ______________________
3. ______________________
4. ______________________
5. ______________________

Name ______________________ Date ______________ Class ______________

Vocabulary Power

Review: Unit 1

EXERCISE

Circle the letter of the word that best completes the sentence.

1. When a person is confused, he or she is in a state of _______.
   a. endeavor b. anticipation c. nurture d. bewilderment

2. If you resent a decrease in your allowance, you may be _______.
   a. hostile b. emphatic c. mortified d. engaging

3. Growing up requires the ability to _______.
   a. emphasize b. embroider c. endorse d. cope

4. Self- _______ is an important quality to develop.
   a. reliance b. anticipation c. defiance d. bewilderment

5. When the _______ sounded, the students filed out.
   a. pang b. kindred c. alarm d. edifice

6. A church is an example of a(n) _______.
   a. resident b. edifice c. vicinity d. sentiment

7. Opposition to the dam project helped join the townspeople in a(n) _______ cause.
   a. communal b. unique c. emphatic d. mortified

8. He was surprised to _______ poverty in a rich city.
   a. envelop b. endeavor c. encounter d. employ

9. In _______ of victory, the candidate threw a party.
   a. bewilderment b. defiance c. alarm d. anticipation

10. Going alone to Europe was a(n) _______ experience for her.
    a. communal b. emphatic c. unique d. mortified

Name _______________ Date _______________ Class _______________

Vocabulary Power

Test: Unit 1

PART A

Circle the letter of the word that best completes the sentence.

1. The lieutenant thought that it was a bad idea to enter ______ territory.
   a. emphatic b. hostile c. communal d. mortified

2. The two were so much alike that everyone called them ______ spirits.
   a. hostile b. edifice c. kindred d. resident

3. The crime took place in the ______ of Oak Road and West Avenue.
   a. vicinity b. sentiment c. reliance d. anticipation

4. The mail carrier ______ many different people as she walked her route.
   a. endeavored b. dwelled c. enabled d. encountered

5. The company ______ two new computer technicians.
   a. resented b. employed c. enabled d. coped

6. During the debate, the most popular mayoral candidate ______ the issue of education.
   a. nurtured b. enveloped c. emphasized d. endeavored

7. She bought a new outfit in ______ of her dinner date.
   a. defiance b. reliance c. bewilderment d. anticipation

8. The audience responded positively to the speaker's ______ smile.
   a. engaging b. emphatic c. communal d. hostile

9. The writer ______ the criticism leveled at his book.
   a. employed b. enveloped c. resented d. enabled

10. To show her ______, the girl refused to eat her supper.
    a. bewilderment b. vicinity c. defiance d. reliance

PART B

Circle the letter of the best answer to each question.

1. What is an example of your ability to cope with a conflict in a friendship?
   a. avoiding your friend
   b. asking for a chance to talk out the situation, in the presence of a counselor, if need be
   c. creating a scene
   d. gossiping behind your friend's back

Vocabulary Power *continued*

2. What is a synonym for *mortified?*
   a. embarrassed
   b. embalmed
   c. embraced
   d. embroidered

3. What might alarm a person?
   a. a rainbow
   b. a friendly letter
   c. a sunny day
   d. a sudden loud noise

4. How would a person be likely to react to a bewildering situation?
   a. with pity
   b. with anger
   c. with puzzlement
   d. with joy

5. What is an example of emphatic language?
   a. Well, maybe so.
   b. No! Definitely not!
   c. Perhaps.
   d. I imagine.

6. Which of the following is an edifice?
   a. a swift current
   b. a Web site
   c. a candy counter
   d. a law building

PART C

Circle the letter of the word that is most nearly *opposite* in meaning.

1. nurture
   a. promote b. neglect c. understand d. limit

2. defiance
   a. obedience b. challenge c. anger d. sadness

3. endorse
   a. support b. relate c. recommend d. criticize

4. communal
   a. equal b. holy c. private d. shared

Name ______________________ Date ______________ Class ______________

Vocabulary Power

Lesson 5 Using Context Clues

Although animals are different from human beings in many ways, they also share many traits. The words in the following list deal with animals and their personalities, movements, and habitats. Don't be surprised, though, if the words can apply to humans too!

Word List

aquatic	**gait**	**lure**	**shuffle**
cunning	**haughty**	**lurk**	**solitude**
feline	**lair**		

EXERCISE A Context Clues

Study the paragraphs below. Fill in each blank with the word that best fits from the list. Double-check your answers by looking up the meanings of these words in a dictionary.

Always scorning people and her food, Princess the cat is known for being ________________. This morning she emerges from her ________________—a cardboard box filled with soft blankets—and scrutinizes her surroundings.

Her owner begins to ________________ papers at his desk. Then, he spots his cat and tries to ________________ her toward him with a bowl of milk. Princess ignores him and watches that dumb dog Dino trot past her, his ________________ quick and impatient. Panting, his tongue hanging out, Dino pads over to the aquarium to watch the turtle and other ________________ creatures.

Princess doesn't feel like playing any of her ________________ tricks on Dino. Instead, she decides to ________________ in the corner next to the door, waiting for her opportunity to escape the house and be alone, for the one thing that this ________________ loves is her ________________.

EXERCISE B Synonyms

For each group of words and phrases, write the vocabulary word that best fits.

1. watery, oceanic, marine ________________
2. tempt, entice, attract ________________
3. proud, scornful, arrogant ________________
4. clever, sly, tricky ________________
5. sneak, slink, lie in wait ________________

Name ____________________ Date ____________ Class ____________

Vocabulary Power continued

EXERCISE C Multiple-Meanings Words

Several of the words in the list have more than one meaning. The word *shuffle* is an example. Study the meanings listed below for *shuffle* and read the sentences that follow. Determine which meaning of the word is correct for each sentence and, to the left, write in the number of that definition.

shuffle *v.* **1.** to move about this way and that; mix **2.** to rearrange so as to place in random order, as a deck of cards **3.** to walk with a dragging step **4.** to perform, as a dance, with a dragging motion of the feet. **5.** to move back and forth from one place to another

_______ 1. The magician **shuffled** the cards before asking the visitor to choose one.

_______ 2. The banker **shuffled** the accounts from Chicago to Switzerland.

_______ 3. Grandfather **shuffled** over to the kitchen sink to get a drink of water.

_______ 4. The businessman **shuffled** the memos on his desk as he talked to a client.

_______ 5. The tap dancers **shuffled** along the stage in time with the music.

EXERCISE D Usage

If the boldfaced word is used correctly in the sentence, write *correct* above it. If not, draw a line through the word and write the correct vocabulary word above it.

1. The dancers in the musical *Cats* moved with **feline** grace.
2. The lion emerged from his **gait**, rested and ready to hunt.
3. For people tired of the rat race, the perfect vacation spot offers peace and **solitude**.
4. The policeman walked to the scene of the crime with a strong and steady **shuffle**.
5. The store owners **lurk** potential customers away from their competitors with lower prices and free hot dogs.

EXERCISE E Word Illustrations

Think about how the vocabulary words in this list describe or relate to one or two particular animals. On a separate sheet of paper, draw a picture that illustrates the meaning of one or two of the words. Then, write a caption for your drawing using the words you chose.

Name ______________________ Date ______________ Class ______________

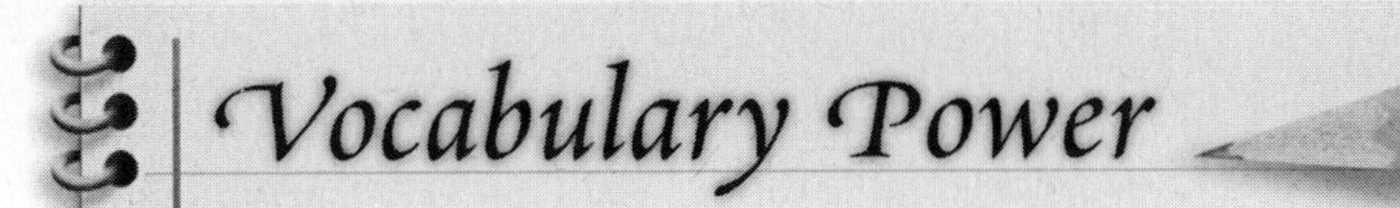

Lesson 6 The Word Roots *homo, humanus, anima, animus, anthropo,* and *bio*

The root part of a word carries the word's main meaning. The vocabulary words in this lesson have one of the following as their roots: *homo* or *humanus, anima* or *animus, anthropo* or *bio. Homo* means "man" and *humanus* means "belonging to a man." *Anima* means "the soul" and *animus* means "the mind." *Anthropos* means "human being," and *bio* means "life."

Word List

amphibious	**antibiotic**	**homogeneous**	**philanthropy**
anthropology	**biology**	**humane**	**unanimous**
animated	**homicide**		

EXERCISE A Etymology

Write down the word you think comes from the Latin words that are given. Then, write your own definition for the word. Double-check your answers in a dictionary.

1. *philos,* which means "loving," plus *anthropos,* which means "human being" ______________

____

2. *anthropos,* which means "human being," plus *logy,* which means "science of" ______________

____

3. *bio,* which means "life," plus *logy,* which means "science of" ______________

____

4. *animare,* which means "to give life to" ______________

____

5. *homo,* which means "man," plus *cida,* which means "to kill" ______________

____

6. *anti,* which means "against," plus *bio,* which means "life" ______________

____

7. *humanus,* which means "belonging to a man" ______________

____

8. *homo,* which means "same," plus *genos,* which means "kind" ______________

____

Name ______________________ Date ______________ Class ______________

Vocabulary Power *continued*

9. *amphi,* which means "on both sides," plus *bio,* which means "life" ______________________

____

10. *unus,* which means "one," plus *animus,* which means "mind" ______________________

____

EXERCISE B Usage

If the boldfaced word is used correctly in the sentence, write *correct* above it. If not, draw a line through the word and write the correct vocabulary word above it.

1. Because she enjoyed studying the science of human beings, especially their classifications, origins, and cultures, the college student was majoring in **philanthropy**.
2. Frogs are **amphibious,** which means they can live on land and in water.
3. Gesturing wildly and speaking loudly, the two men were engaged in a(n) **homogeneous** conversation.
4. Her fascination with all living things led her to work in the field of **biology**.
5. The defendant was charged with **homicide** and sentenced to life in prison.
6. The gardener used the **antibiotic** ointment on her cut.
7. Even though she isn't rich, my grandmother has a spirit of **philanthropy**.
8. The veterinarian thought that putting the sick animal to sleep was the **unanimous** thing to do.

EXERCISE C Solving a Word Puzzle

For each word or phrase, write in the vocabulary word that best fits. Then, unscramble the circled letters to find the answer to the question.

1. study of living things ___ (___) ___ ___ (___)(___) ___

2. lively ___ (___) ___ ___ (___) ___ ___ (___)

3. able to live on land and sea ___ (___)(___)(___) ___ ___ ___ ___ ___ ___ ___

Question: How did the frog react when his friend pushed him off the lily pad?

Answer: He was ___ ___ ___ P ___ ___ ___   ___ ___ ___

Name ______________________ Date ______________ Class ______________

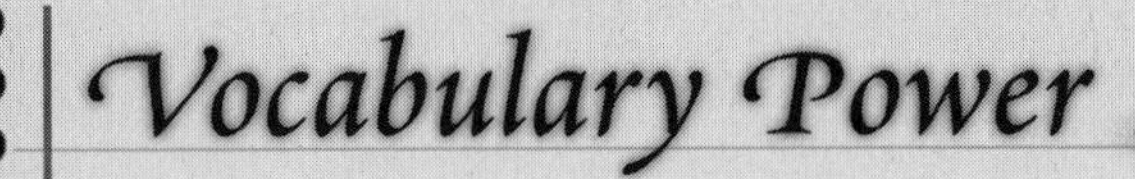

Lesson 7 Word Usage

Animals could not survive without plants. The vocabulary words in the following list have to do with plants and animals.

Word List

apiary	**burrow**	**habitat**	**terrarium**
arboreal	**carnivorous**	**reap**	**zoology**
botany	**cultivate**		

EXERCISE A Usage

Fill in each blank with the word from the list that best fits. Double-check your answers by looking up the meanings of these words in a dictionary.

1. If you like plants, you should study ______________, but if you like animals, you should study ______________.
2. The place in which an animal lives is called its ______________.
3. An animal that lives in the trees can be described as ______________.
4. Farmers first ______________ their crops and then ______________ the harvest.
5. Rabbits ______________ in the ground for shelter from ______________ animals, which would attack and eat them.
6. Human beings sometimes keep plants and small animals in their homes in a(n) ______________.
7. A beekeeper often spends many hours in the ______________ tending to the bees.

EXERCISE B Context Clues

Write the vocabulary word that best matches the clue.

1. Someone who is allergic to bee stings would probably stay far away from this. ______________
2. This word describes monkeys and squirrels. ______________
3. Woodchucks like to do this. ______________
4. This is a glass-enclosed place for plants and small animals. ______________
5. This is another word for harvest. ______________

Vocabulary Power *continued*

EXERCISE C Etymology

Fill in the vocabulary word that best completes each sentence.

1. Knowing that the Latin *carn-* means "flesh" and *vorare* means "to devour" can help you to understand the meaning of the word ________________.
2. The word for the study of plants, ________________, is based on the Greek word *botanikos.*
3. Knowing that the Latin word *habitare* means "to dwell" helps you with the meaning of the word ________________.
4. The word ________________ is based on the Latin word *arbor,* which means "a tree."

EXERCISE D Synonyms

For each group of words and phrases, write the vocabulary word that best fits.

1. raise, nurture, grow ________________
2. dwelling place, environment, home ________________
3. dig, hide, nestle ________________
4. obtain, harvest, acquire ________________

EXERCISE E Usage

On a separate sheet of paper, write a sentence for each vocabulary word using the word correctly. The sentences should show that you understand the word's meaning.

Name ______________________ Date ______________ Class ______________

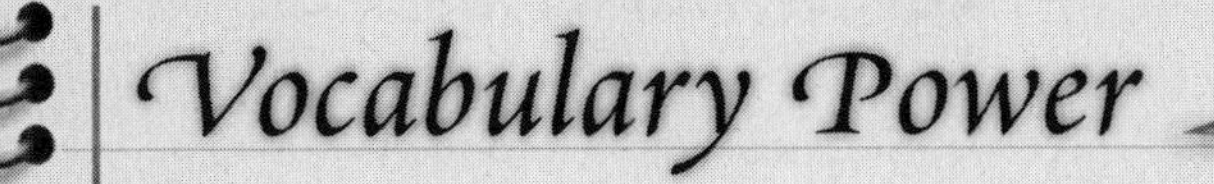

Lesson 8 The Latin Roots *movere* and *mobilis*

Familiar words such as *movie* and *motor* originate in the Latin root *movere.* The words in the Word List are based either on *movere* or *mobilis,* which means "easily moved."

Word List			
commotion	**mobile**	**momentum**	**promote**
demote	**momentary**	**motive**	**remote**
immobilize	**momentous**		

EXERCISE A Synonyms

Each boldfaced vocabulary word is paired with a synonym whose meaning you probably know. Think of other words related to the meaning of the synonym and write your ideas on the line provided. Then, write the dictionary definition of the vocabulary word.

1. **commotion** : agitation ______________________

   Dictionary definition ______________________

2. **demote** : reduce ______________________

   Dictionary definition ______________________

3. **immobilize** : to make motionless ______________________

   Dictionary definition ______________________

4. **mobile** : movable ______________________

   Dictionary definition ______________________

5. **momentary** : fleeting ______________________

   Dictionary definition ______________________

6. **momentous** : important ______________________

   Dictionary definition ______________________

7. **momentum** : force ______________________

   Dictionary definition ______________________

8. **motive** : reason ______________________

   Dictionary definition ______________________

9. **promote** : advance ______________________

   Dictionary definition ______________________

Name ______________________ Date ______________ Class ______________

Vocabulary Power *continued*

10. **remote** : distant ______________________

Dictionary definition ______________________

EXERCISE B Antonyms

Write the vocabulary word that is most nearly *opposite* in meaning.

1. stillness ______________
2. unimportant ______________
3. discourage ______________
4. advance ______________
5. immovable ______________
6. move ______________
7. long-lived ______________
8. near ______________

EXERCISE C Multiple-Meaning Words

Several of the words in this word list have more than one meaning. Fill in the blanks with the word that best completes each sentence. To the left of each sentence, write the number of the definition that best fits.

> **promote** *v.* **1.** to advance in station, rank, or honor; elevate **2.** to help develop or establish: further **3.** to further the sale of (an item or service) through advertising
> **remote** *adj.* **1.** far away in distance **2.** secluded **3.** slight **4.** controlled indirectly from a distance **5.** distant in manner: uninterested

_____ **1.** The two brothers fought over who would use the television's ______________ control.

_____ **2.** The army did not ______________ the corporal to the rank of sergeant.

_____ **3.** There is only a ______________ possibility that the popular singer will hold a concert in our town.

_____ **4.** Sending troops to such a ______________ country would require a huge investment of personnel, time, and money.

_____ **5.** The hermit emerges from his ______________ dwelling only once or twice a year.

_____ **6.** The company decided to ______________ its new product mainly through television commercials.

_____ **7.** The teacher uses many innovative techniques to ______________ learning in her classroom.

EXERCISE D Usage

On a separate sheet of paper, write a paragraph or two in which you use each of the words in the list correctly. The paragraphs should show that you understand each vocabulary word's meaning.

Name ______________________ Date ______________ Class ____________

Lesson 9 Using Reading Skills

Using Context Clues

When you read an unfamiliar word in a sentence, do you stop and immediately look the word up in the dictionary? Chances are that you might first try to guess the meaning of the word from the *context,* or the sentence or group of sentences in which the word appears. Words that provide hints as to the meaning of another word are called *context clues.*

There are different kinds of context clues. For example, sometimes the unknown word might be defined within the sentence:

The dog was ecstatic–simply overjoyed–when his owner came home.

Sometimes, you may get an idea of the word's meaning because the meaning is restated in a different way:

The dog was ecstatic when his owner, Mrs. Juarez, came home. He simply could not contain his delight.

And, sometimes, the unknown word is contrasted with another word or phrase whose meaning is familiar:

It seems that lately the dog has been either ecstatic at Mrs. Juarez's return, or just the opposite–disinterested.

To use context clues in determining the meaning of an unknown word, first read the sentence carefully for the kinds of clues described above. Then, when you think you know the word's definition, replace the unknown word with your definition. Does it make sense? Finally, check your definition in the dictionary.

EXERCISE

Use context clues to figure out the meaning of each boldfaced word. Follow the steps described above. Then, write your definition for each word.

1. The cautious young man was very **circumspect** with his hard-earned money. ______________
____
2. The woman thought her husband was too **miserly**–she had to account for every penny she spent.
____
3. The moon was **luminous** that night–it lit up the whole sky. ______________
____
4. The student took **copious** notes–she wrote so much that her hand hurt. ______________
____
5. The lawyer seemed to have two different personalities: sometimes he was **playful**; at other times, extremely serious. ______________
6. There was no way that the troops were going to **relinquish** their weapons. They would not give up without a fight. ______________

Name ______________________ Date ______________ Class ______________

Vocabulary Power

Review: Unit 2

EXERCISE

Circle the letter of the word that best completes each sentence.

1. The study of plants is known as ______.
   a. anthropology b. botany c. zoology d. philanthropy
2. The doctor told the boy that she would have to ______ his wrist so that he couldn't damage it by movement.
   a. promote b. lure c. immobilize d. shuffle
3. After hours of polite banter, Mr. Peacock left the party to find ______.
   a. momentum b. commotion c. solitude d. motive
4. The fisher wanted to ______ the biggest fish in the pond onto his hook.
   a. lure b. lurk c. reap d. demote
5. The ______ thief tricked the homeowner into opening her door.
   a. momentary b. homogeneous c. mobile d. cunning
6. After years of careful planning and saving, the retired couple were going to ______ the benefits of their efforts.
   a. promote b. reap c. immobilize d. burrow
7. A lion is one example of a(n) ______ animal.
   a. feline b. amphibious c. unanimous d. momentary
8. Many animal rights activists work to encourage the ______ treatment of animals.
   a. apiary b. humane c. haughty d. remote
9. The farmer decided to ______ a wide variety of crops this year.
   a. remote b. immobilize c. burrow d. cultivate
10. A(n) ______ speaker, the doctor kept the audience riveted to their seats.
    a. antibiotic b. mobile c. animated d. momentary

Name ______________________ Date ______________ Class __________

Vocabulary Power

Test: Unit 2

PART A

Circle the letter of the word that best completes the sentence.

1. After months of declining sales, the vice president of sales was _______ to regional manager.
   a. reaped b. immobilized c. demoted d. burrowed

2. Police statistics show that the number of _______ has decreased.
   a. homicides b. lairs c. felines d. philanthropies

3. The horse trotted around the track with a strong and steady _______.
   a. motive b. commotion c. gait d. habitat

4. The boy _______ his feet as the coach corrected him.
   a. lured b. shuffled c. cultivated d. promoted

5. Her arm became increasingly _______ as she worked with a physical therapist.
   a. haughty b. arboreal c. carnivorous d. mobile

6. The big truck gained _______ as it rolled down the hill.
   a. terrarium b. momentary c. motive d. momentum

7. The people who lived in the _______ village had to walk miles for safe drinking water.
   a. momentous b. remote c. arboreal d. cunning

8. The gardener added a few plants to her _______ every year.
   a. terrarium b. lair c. botany d. motive

9. Tired of living in _______, the man bought a kitten and a puppy.
   a. apiary b. commotion c. solitude d. philanthropy

10. The lifeguard excelled at _______ sports such as swimming and water skiing.
    a. antibiotic b. unanimous c. apiary d. aquatic

PART B

Answer *yes* or *no* to each question and briefly explain your answer.

1. If your classmates are participating in an animated discussion about the school dance, are they probably bored?

   ____

Name ______________________ Date ______________ Class __________

Vocabulary Power *continued*

2. If an inexperienced worker goes to work in an apiary, should he or she wear protective gear?

____

3. If you want to cultivate a friendship with Jane, the new student, should you ignore her?

____

4. Is a lake the natural habitat of an alligator?

____

5. If your school council reaches a unanimous decision about a free day, do you think the members had a hard time agreeing?

____

6. If your uncle has an arboreal job, is he likely to work outdoors?

____

7. If an animal is carnivorous, does it eat flesh?

____

8 If you are interested in plant life, would you major in botany?

____

9. If commotion occurs regularly in the library, is it a good place for you to study?

____

10. Is your motive logical if you want to learn mathematics so that you can be a financial advisor later?

____

Name ____________________ Date ______________ Class ________

Vocabulary Power

Lesson 10 Usage

Growing up can be both painful and enjoyable. The words in the following list deal with the aches and rewards of growing up. How many of these words can you apply to your life?

Word List

aptitude	**laughingstock**	**reflective**	**sulk**
forlorn	**limelight**	**squabble**	**superb**
impudent	**mingle**		

EXERCISE A Sentence Completion

Fill in each blank below with the word from the list that best completes the sentence. Check your answers by looking up the meaning of these words in a dictionary.

1. After Mitsuyo opened her diary, she was ______________, quietly thinking about the day's events.
2. Frank, who loved to be the center of attention, was always seeking the ______________.
3. Realizing that she had a(n) ______________ for math, Meg decided to make it her major area of study.
4. Soaked and shivering, the little puppy looked ______________ out in the rain by itself.
5. The restaurant critic gave Mario's restaurant a(n) ______________ review and four stars.
6. After her ______________ remark, Tori was sent to the principal's office.
7. After running the wrong way in the football game, Ken thought that he would be the ______________ of the whole school.
8. Jenny crossed her arms, closed her mouth tightly, and began to ______________ about missing the sleepover at her friend's house.
9. At the party, Mrs. Ramirez tried to ______________ with the other managers and their families.
10. The parents told their children that if they continued to ______________ over the remote control, the TV would be turned off.

Name ______________________ Date ______________ Class ____________

Vocabulary Power *continued*

EXERCISE B Synonyms

After each group of words and phrases, write the vocabulary word that best fits.

1. talent, tendency, intelligence ______________
2. rude, contemptuous, bold ______________
3. argue, fight, quarrel ______________
4. abandoned, forsaken, dejected ______________

EXERCISE C Context Clues

Write the vocabulary word that best matches the clue.

1. People who don't get their own way sometimes do this instead of arguing. ______________
2. Movie stars might enjoy basking in this. ______________
3. Someone who makes a fool out of himself or herself may be considered this. ______________
4. A welcome guest can do this with apparent ease. ______________
5. Best of the best ______________
6. A person who thinks about past experiences is this. ______________

EXERCISE D Usage

Think about how the vocabulary words relate to growing up. Then, write a letter to a friend in which you use all of the words. You might write about an event that actually happened or about an imaginary event. Your letter should show that you understand the meaning of each vocabulary word.

Name ______________________ Date ______________ Class ______________

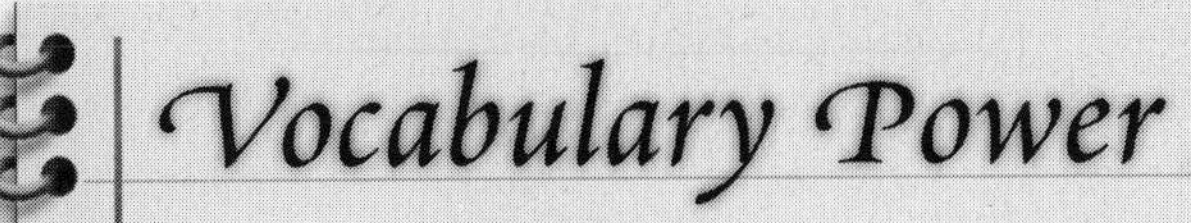

Vocabulary Power

Lesson 11 Usage

Have you ever watched a television news story about a war? The newscaster most likely used words often associated with conflict. The words in the following list can be used not only in wartime but also during peacetime.

Word List

amass	**hover**	**meager**	**retreat**
camouflage	**intrigue**	**procession**	**treacherous**
conquest	**jargon**		

EXERCISE A Sentence Completion

Fill in the blanks below with words from the list that best fit. Double-check your answers by looking up the meanings of these words in a dictionary.

1. The funeral ________________ filed silently by Aunt Emma's house.
2. The ________________ of the Aztec Indians by Cortez occurred in the early 1500s.
3. The sign read "Beware of ________________ footing on the cliff-face."
4. Anita had to ________________ from standing so near the fireplace.
5. Their ________________ provisions were not enough to get them through the week.
6. Lauren had a lot of technical ________________ to learn at her new job.
7. If you invest wisely while you are young, you can ________________ a fortune for retirement.
8. Jim put on his ________________ in preparation for the paintball tournament.
9. James Bond lives in a world of ________________ and deception.
10. The helicoper pilot had to ________________ over the boat for ten minutes.

EXERCISE B Usage

If the boldfaced word is used correctly in the sentence, write *correct* above it. If not, draw a line through the word and write the correct vocabulary word above it.

1. In presenting the program, the computer expert used so much **conquest** that the class could not understand.
2. The **retreat** of red ants carrying crumbs inched up the hill.
3. People across the city began to **hover** canned goods and other necessities in preparation for the big winter storm.

Vocabulary Power continued

4. As a result of the **meager** rainfall this summer, vegetables and fruits have been expensive.

5. The freezing rain caused **treacherous** driving conditions.

EXERCISE C Antonyms

Write the vocabulary word that is most nearly *opposite* in meaning.

1. abundant ______________
2. distribute ______________
3. defeat ______________
4. advance ______________
5. loyal ______________

EXERCISE D Multiple-Meaning Words

Several words in the list have more than one meaning. Fill in the blanks with the words that best complete the sentences. In the space next to each sentence, write the number of the definition that helped you make your choice.

hover *v.* **1.** to hang fluttering in the air **2.** to move back and forth near a place; wait nearby **3.** to be in an uncertain state
intrigue *v.* **1.** to cheat, trick **2.** to accomplish by intrigue **3.** to arouse the interest, desire, or curiosity of

_______ 1. Officer Fox told the pilot of the news helicopter not to ______________ directly above the scene of the crime.

_______ 2. The writers of the movie script created a plot they hoped would ______________ viewers.

_______ 3. Just before walking down the aisle, the bride ______________(ed) between happiness and panic.

_______ 4. The prisoner thought his ______________ was foolproof.

_______ 5. The grandparents ______________(ed) at the door of the delivery room, eager to see their first grandchild.

EXERCISE E Usage

On a separate sheet of paper, write sentences in which you use each of the words in the list correctly. The sentences should show that you understand the word's meaning.

Name ______________________ Date ______________ Class __________

Vocabulary Power

Lesson 12 The Latin Roots *scribere* and *signare*

The root part of a word carries the word's main meaning. The vocabulary words in this lesson have to do with writing or marking. These words have one of the following as their root: the Latin *scribere,* which means "to write," or *signare,* which means "to mark."

Word List

circumscribe	**inscription**	**resigned**	**subscribe**
conscription	**insignia**	**significant**	**transcribe**
designate	**nondescript**		

EXERCISE A Synonyms

Each boldfaced vocabulary word is paired with a synonym whose meaning you probably know. Think of other words related to the meaning of the synonym and write your ideas on the line provided. Then, look up the vocabulary word in the dictionary and write its meaning.

1. **circumscribe** : surround ______________________

   Dictionary definition ______________________

2. **conscription** : draft ______________________

   Dictionary definition ______________________

3. **designate** : name ______________________

   Dictionary definition ______________________

4. **inscription** : engraving ______________________

   Dictionary definition ______________________

5. **insignia** : medal ______________________

   Dictionary definition ______________________

6. **nondescript** : unremarkable ______________________

   Dictionary definition ______________________

7. **resigned** : accepting ______________________

   Dictionary definition ______________________

8. **significant** : important ______________________

   Dictionary definition ______________________

Vocabulary Power continued

9. **subscribe** : sign up for ______________________________

   Dictionary definition ______________________________

10. **transcribe** : copy ______________________________

    Dictionary definition ______________________________

EXERCISE B Synonyms

For each group of words and phrases, write the vocabulary word that best fits.

1. name, nominate, elect ______________
2. important, weighty, noticeable ______________
3. emblem, symbol, medal ______________
4. uninteresting, dull, unremarkable ______________

EXERCISE C Context Clues

Write the vocabulary word that best matches the clue.

1. A military draft is often called this. ______________
2. This might read "To My Dear Wife" and appear on the back of a locket. ______________
3. You do this if you want to receive a certain magazine every month. ______________
4. A police officer's badge is an example of this. ______________
5. A movie star who doesn't want to be recognized might wear this kind of clothing. ______________

EXERCISE D Word Puzzle

For each word or phrase, write in the vocabulary word that best fits. Then, unscramble the circled letters to solve the riddle.

1. to draw a circle around __ __ (__) __ __ __ __ __ __ (__) __ __
2. to translate __ __ __ (__) __ __ __ __ __ (__)
3. to name (__) (__) (__) __ (__) __ __ __ __ __

   Question: How did the man feel when he realized he had lost his new jacket?

   Answer: He was __ __ __ __ __ __ __ __

Name ______________________ Date ____________ Class ____________

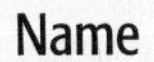

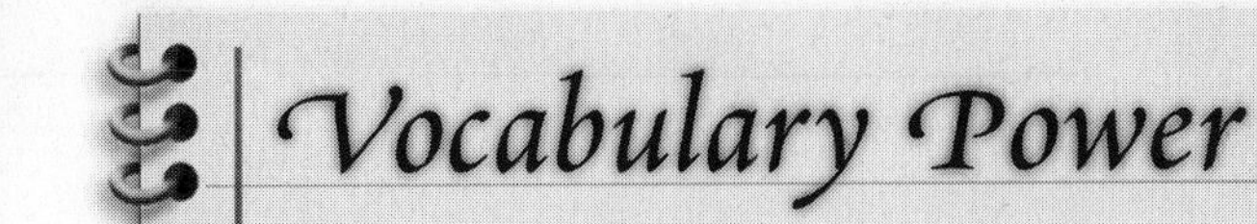

Lesson 13 Using Reference Skills

Finding the Right Definition

Have you ever looked up an unfamiliar word in the dictionary only to find more than one definition? How did you know which definition to choose? The following guidelines can guide you to the right definition in the dictionary.

1. First, read all of the definitions provided. For example, suppose that you came across the following sentence:

   The nurse told the patient that the thermometer *registered* 101°F.

   If you are unfamiliar with the word *register,* the next step would be to look up the word in a dictionary. The following is an example of the dictionary entry for the word *register.*

> **register** (rej′ ə ster) *v.* **1.** to write or record officially **2.** to enroll, as a student or a voter **3.** to make a note of **4.** to record automatically; to indicate **5.** to show an emotion by one's actions or facial expression *n.* **1.** a printed or written record or list **2.** a book in which a written record is kept **3.** a machine or device that automatically counts or records **4.** the range of a musical instrument or voice **5.** an opening in the floor or wall that allows heated or cooled air to pass through **6.** in printing, the exact alignment of lines, colors, and so on

2. Next, determine which definition you need by replacing the word you looked up with each of its definitions. You can immediately eliminate a definition for a different part of speech. In the above example, you know that *register* is a verb because it performs an action. Therefore, you know that you cannot choose any of the definitions that are nouns.

   Now you need to try out the definitions that are verbs. Whichever definition makes the most sense within the context of the sentence is the correct definition.

   The nurse told the patient that the thermometer *indicated* 101°F.

EXERCISE

Look up the boldfaced word in each sentence. Decide which dictionary definition you think is correct and write the correct definition.

1. The shopper **redeemed** his coupons at the grocery store for cash. ______________________

____

2. After gossiping about a classmate, the boy **redeemed** his action by telling the class he had lied. ________

____

3. The cancer patient was beginning to **recover**. ______________________

____

4. The homeowners could not **recover** the items that were stolen from their house. ____________

____

5. The elderly man was the **original** owner of the house. ______________________

____

Name ______________________ Date ______________ Class ______________

Vocabulary Power

Review: Unit 3

EXERCISE

Circle the letter of the word that best completes each sentence.

1. Claiming victory at the press conference, the general described his army's final ______.
   a. jargon b. procession c. conquest d. aptitude

2. Ever since she was a little girl, the actress had always wanted to be in the ______.
   a. insignia b. limelight c. retreat d. laughingstock

3. The shy employee stood in the corner, afraid to ______ with the other guests.
   a. mingle b. transcribe c. amass d. sulk

4. The coaches voted to ______ the shortstop of the Angels as the Most Valuable Player in the league.
   a. circumscribe b. squabble c. subscribe d. designate

5. The mayor was concerned about the ______ increase in crime in her city.
   a. meager b. significant c. resigned d. reflective

6. To hide their position, the soldiers tried to ______ their vehicle with tree branches.
   a. intrigue b. retreat c. camouflage d. squabble

7. The music reviewer highly praised the ______ performance by the visiting orchestra.
   a. forlorn b. superb c. impudent d. resigned

8. The high school teacher had always shown a(n) ______ for helping others learn.
   a. aptitude b. insignia c. conscription d. procession

9. The instructor told the parents not to ______ in the doorway while their children took the test.
   a. designate b. hover c. subscribe d. circumscribe

10. The hikers moved slowly and carefully as they crossed a particularly ______ part of the mountain.
    a. nondescript b. reflective c. treacherous d. impudent

Name ______________________ Date ______________ Class ______________

Vocabulary Power

Test: Unit 3

PART A

Circle the letter of the word that best completes each sentence.

1. The sisters _______ loudly over who got to ride in the front seat.
   a. subscribed b. squabbled c. retreated d. resigned

2. The parents could not understand the doctor because of his medical _______.
   a. procession b. conscription c. jargon d. limelight

3. The girl _______ all evening because her parents refused to let her go to the party.
   a. sulked b. camouflaged c. circumscribed d. mingled

4. After arriving at the cemetery, the first car in the funeral _______ stopped at the grave site.
   a. insignia b. conquest c. conscription d. procession

5. The husband told the jeweler that he wanted a special _______ on the back of the locket he bought for his wife's fortieth birthday.
   a. inscription b. limelight c. laughingstock d. intrigue

6. The eyewitnesses found it difficult to give police a description of the bank robber because his clothing was so _______.
   a. significant b. nondescript c. reflective d. treacherous

7. At an early age, the orator showed a(n) _______ for speaking.
   a. insignia b. retreat c. aptitude d. conscription

8. With supplies running low, the soldiers ate only one _______ meal a day.
   a. superb b. resigned c. meager d. impudent

9. The helicopter pilot tried to _______ over the burning building, but the heat was too intense.
   a. hover b. transcribe c. subscribe d. designate

10. The doctor was _______ by the recession of the disease.
    a. mingled b. resigned c. intrigued d. amassed

Name ______________________________ Date ________________ Class ____________

Vocabulary Power *continued*

PART B

Circle the letter of the answer that correctly completes each sentence.

1. Before a squabble could erupt between the children, Mr. Dolenz ______.
   - a. ate his tie
   - b. rode into the sunset
   - c. started to play a videogame
   - d. had them work in separate areas

2. If you subscribe to the way your parents treat you, you probably ______.
   - a. oppose their views
   - b. support their views
   - c. send them monthly subscription fees
   - d. ignore your parents

3. Many animals have a natural camouflage that enables them to ______.
   - a. escape heavy rain
   - b. keep their hides smooth and sleek
   - c. scent out adversaries
   - d. escape detection

4. If your relatives have amassed a fortune, they have ______ money.
   - a. accumulated
   - b. lost
   - c. been sent
   - d. given away

5. An insignia showing a panda served as a ______.
   - a. conversation point
   - b. toy shop advertisement
   - c. reminder of the endangered species
   - d. photo ready for framing

PART C

Circle the letter of the word that is most nearly *opposite* in meaning.

1. **superb**
   a. good b. angry c. awful d. first

2. **impudent**
   a. respectful b. intelligent c. clean d. clear

3. **resigned**
   a. depressed b. rebellious c. luxurious d. distant

4. **subscribe**
   a. anger b. disapprove c. forget d. disappoint

5. **treacherous**
   a. difficult b. generous c. depressed d. safe

Name ______________________ Date ______________ Class ____________

Vocabulary Power

Lesson 14 Using Synonyms

Different people value different things. However, some values remain the same from one generation to the next and from one culture to the next. The words in the following list have to do with how our values influence our thoughts, emotions, words, and deeds.

Word List

blissful	**deceptive**	**hoard**	**squander**
compassion	**discreet**	**solace**	**vain**
consequence	**heed**		

EXERCISE A Synonyms

Each boldfaced vocabulary word is paired with a synonym whose meaning you probably know. Think of other words related to the synonym and write them on the line provided. Then, look up the vocabulary word in a dictionary and write its meaning.

1. **blissful** : joyful ______________________

   Dictionary definition ______________________

2. **compassion** : sympathy ______________________

   Dictionary definition ______________________

3. **consequence** : result ______________________

   Dictionary definition ______________________

4. **deceptive** : misleading ______________________

   Dictionary definition ______________________

5. **discreet** : careful ______________________

   Dictionary definition ______________________

6. **heed** : mind ______________________

   Dictionary definition ______________________

7. **hoard** : collect ______________________

   Dictionary definition ______________________

8. **solace** : relief ______________________

   Dictionary definition ______________________

Vocabulary Power *continued*

9. **squander** : waste ______________________

   Dictionary definition ______________________

10. **vain** : worthless ______________________

   Dictionary definition ______________________

EXERCISE B Usage

If the boldfaced word is used correctly in the sentence, write *correct* above it. If not, draw a line through the word and write the correct vocabulary word above it.

1. The **discreet** psychiatrist never shared information regarding his patients.
2. Showing **consequence** for the girl who forgot her lunch, members of the class gave her some of their own.
3. She made a desperate attempt to catch the plane, but it was in **hoard** as the plane was already taxiing down the runway.
4. The lifeguard told the swimmers to **squander** his words about swimming safety.
5. The little girl's parents gave her **solace** after her cat died.

EXERCISE C Context Clues

Write the vocabulary word that best matches the clue.

1. Can describe chocolate lovers in a fudge shop. ______________
2. What you should do with a wise person's advice. ______________
3. Compulsive gamblers often do this with their money. ______________
4. Friends and family offer this to one another in times of grief. ______________
5. Describes a magician's tricks. ______________
6. Squirrels do this with nuts to prepare for the winter. ______________

Name ______________________ Date ______________ Class ____________

Vocabulary Power

Lesson 15 The Latin Root *verto*

The root part of a word carries the word's main meaning. The vocabulary words in this lesson share the Latin root *verto,* which comes from the word *vertere,* meaning "to turn."

Word List

adversary	**controversy**	**extroverted**	**universal**
aversion	**convert**	**traverse**	**versatile**
avert	**diversion**		

EXERCISE A Synonyms

Each boldfaced vocabulary word is paired with a synonym whose meaning you probably know. Think of other related words and write them on the line provided. Then, look up the vocabulary word in a dictionary and write its meaning.

1. **adversary** : enemy ______________________

   Dictionary definition ______________________

2. **aversion** : dislike ______________________

   Dictionary definition ______________________

3. **avert** : deflect ______________________

   Dictionary definition ______________________

4. **controversy** : dispute ______________________

   Dictionary definition ______________________

5. **convert** : transform ______________________

   Dictionary definition ______________________

6. **diversion** : pastime ______________________

   Dictionary definition ______________________

7. **extroverted** : outgoing ______________________

   Dictionary definition ______________________

8. **traverse** : cross ______________________

   Dictionary definition ______________________

Vocabulary Power *continued*

9. **universal** : general ______________________

   Dictionary definition ______________________

10. **versatile** : adaptable ______________________

   Dictionary definition ______________________

EXERCISE B Context Clues

Write the vocabulary word that best matches the clue.

1. You wouldn't be friendly with a person who is this. ______________
2. You do this to get from one side of a bridge to another. ______________
3. This kind of person is most likely to be the life of the party. ______________
4. You do this with your eyes if you don't want to look at something. ______________
5. Something shared by everyone is this. ______________
6. Another word for *dispute*. ______________

EXERCISE C Usage

If the boldfaced word is used correctly in the sentence, write *correct* above it. If it is not, draw a line through the word and write the correct vocabulary word above it.

1. The boy who was allergic to bee stings had a(n) **diversion** to bees.
2. Mr. Chang bought the jacket because it was so **extroverted**: one side served as a windbreaker, the reverse side could be worn as a raincoat, and the hood could be zipped on and off.
3. The vacationers tried to **avert** disaster by driving home before the hurricane hit the shore.
4. The enthusiastic bicyclists attempted to **convert** the country with only their bikes and their backpacks.
5. The mayor tried to keep her name out of the **controversy** over the misuse of city taxes.
6. A white flag is a(n) **universal** symbol for surrender.

EXERCISE D Usage

On a separate sheet of paper, write sentences in which you use each of the words in the list correctly. The sentences should show that you understand the meaning of each vocabulary word.

Name ______________________ Date ______________ Class ____________

Vocabulary Power

Lesson 16 The Prefix *de-*

Prefixes change the meaning of the roots to which they are added. All of the vocabulary words in the following list have the prefix *de-*. Some meanings of this prefix include "down," "away," and "remove." The prefix *de-* can also serve to make the word root stronger.

Word List

deception	**dehydrated**	**delinquent**	**denounce**
deduce	**dejection**	**delude**	**depleted**
default	**deliberate**		

EXERCISE A Synonyms

Each boldfaced vocabulary word is paired with a synonym whose meaning you probably know. Think of other related words and write them on the line provided. Then, look up the vocabulary word in a dictionary and write its meaning.

1. **deception** : trickery ______________________

   Dictionary definition ______________________

2. **deduce** : conclude ______________________

   Dictionary definition ______________________

3. **default** : fail ______________________

   Dictionary definition ______________________

4. **dehydrated** : dry ______________________

   Dictionary definition ______________________

5. **dejection** : sadness ______________________

   Dictionary definition ______________________

6. **deliberate** : careful ______________________

   Dictionary definition ______________________

7. **delinquent** : overdue ______________________

   Dictionary definition ______________________

8. **delude** : fool ______________________

   Dictionary definition ______________________

9. **denounce** : condemn ______________________

   Dictionary definition ______________________

10. **depleted** : decreased ______________________

   Dictionary definition ______________________

EXERCISE B Etymology

Following are the Latin or Greek words on which some of the vocabulary words are based, along with their meanings. The prefix *de-* affixed to each word has many different meanings. For each Latin or Greek word and definition listed below, write the vocabulary word that you think is related to it. Then, write down another word that might also be based on the Latin or Greek words listed. Look up these words in a dictionary to see if you are right.

1. *de-* plus *nuntiare,* which means "to announce" ______________________
2. *de-* plus *hydor* which means "water" ______________________
3. *de-* plus *fallere,* which means "to fail" ______________________
4. *de-* plus *ducere,* which means "to lead" ______________________
5. *de-* plus *jacere,* which means "to throw" ______________________
6. *de-* plus *plere,* which means "to fill" ______________________
7. *de-* plus *ludere,* which means "to play" ______________________
8. *de-* plus *libra,* which means "a balance" ______________________

EXERCISE C Multiple-Meaning Words

Several of the words in the list have more than one meaning. Fill in each blank below with the word that best completes each sentence. In the space to the left, write the number of the definition that helped you make your choice.

deliberate *v.* **1.** to consider carefully *adj.* **2.** thought out carefully beforehand; done on purpose; intended **3.** slow; unhurried
delinquent: *adj.* **1.** neglecting or failing a duty or obligation, or violating a law **2.** due but not paid; overdue **3.** related to or having to do with delinquents *n.* **4.** a delinquent person

_______ 1. Because the sales manager was _______ in her duties, the company began to lose money.

_______ 2. Not looking forward to the day's trial, the judge took _______ steps up to the courthouse.

_______ 3. After an emotional trial, a jury will _______ on the verdict for several days.

_______ 4. The couple was ordered to pay thousands of dollars in ______________ taxes.

Name ______________________ Date ______________ Class ____________

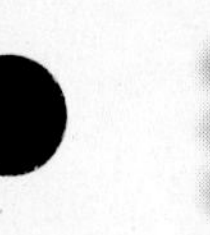

Vocabulary Power

Lesson 17 Using Reading Skills

Understanding Homophones

Can *ewe* find *awl* of the mistakes in this sentence? The mistakes you found are homophones–they sound like other words but are spelled differently and have different meanings. For example, the word *ewe* is pronounced the same as the word *you* but is spelled differently and has a different meaning.

EXERCISE A

For each word below, write in its definition. Then, find a homophone for the word.

1. heal ______________________
2. urn ______________________
3. cymbal ______________________
4. parish ______________________
5. wry ______________________
6. principle ______________________
7. stationary ______________________
8. waive ______________________
9. maul ______________________
10. gilt ______________________

EXERCISE B

If the boldfaced word in each sentence is correct, write *correct* above it. If not, cross out the incorrect word and replace it with the correct homophone.

1. With the elevator broken, Mr. Peterson had to walk up twelve flights of **stares** to his apartment.
2. The mountain climbers grew excited as they neared the **peak.**
3. A fine **missed** sprayed their faces as they approached the powerful waterfall.
4. After their dog died, the family went through a period of **mourning.**
5. Pointing proudly to her parents, the pitcher said that her arm strength came from her **jeans.**
6. The actress **died** her hair brown for her latest role.
7. The groundhog came out of its **hole.**
8. The butcher **wade** the steaks and pork chops on the scale.

Name ______________________ Date ______________ Class ______________

Vocabulary Power

Review: Unit 4

EXERCISE

Circle the letter of the word that best completes each sentence.

1. Although they were ______ on the football field, they were friends off the field.
   a. delinquents b. diversions c. adversaries d. converts

2. Based on the clues, the investigator ______ the identity of the killer.
   a. denounced b. deduced c. traversed d. depleted

3. The politician ______ his opponent's plan to increase taxes to build a new stadium.
   a. extroverted b. solaced c. denounced d. hoarded

4. After being bitten, the boy developed a general ______ to dogs.
   a. aversion b. default c. adversary d. deception

5. As a ______ of studying and working hard, the student received an achievement award in science.
   a. compassion b. convert c. controversy d. consequence

6. Marty is ______ in many mechanical skills, so he is valuable to the company.
   a. extroverted b. versatile c. dehydrated d. delinquent

7. Jane, a sophomore, ______ her grandfather's wise words of advice and stayed in school.
   a. heeded b. hoarded c. defaulted d. converted

8. Instead of saving the money left to him, the young man ______ it all on entertainment and expensive clothes.
   a. averted b. solaced c. squandered d. deluded

9. The jury ______ for only two hours before finding the defendant guilty.
   a. dehydrated b. deliberated c. depleted d. deduced

10. After all of the guests had left, the exhausted hostess stopped to enjoy the ______ sound of silence.
    a. vain b. versatile c. extroverted d. blissful

Name ______________________ Date ______________ Class ______________

Vocabulary Power

Test: Unit 4

PART A

Circle the letter of the word that best completes each sentence.

1. The woman ______ her eyes from the movie screen when the action became too intense.
   a. heeded b. averted c. denounced d. traversed

2. The accountant ______ his living room into a home office.
   a. traversed b. dehydrated c. converted d. deduced

3. Laughter is a ______ sign of happiness.
   a. universal b. deceptive c. vain d. depleted

4. The parents gave ______ to their son when he wasn't chosen to play on the school's basketball team.
   a. consequence b. solace c. deception d. dejection

5. Not wanting to draw attention to herself, the woman tried to be ______ as she left the concert early.
   a. extroverted b. delinquent c. blissful d. discreet

6. The family ______ canned foods in preparation for the coming snowstorm.
   a. hoarded b. denounced c. deliberated d. converted

7. The explorers ______ mountains and deserts in their search for gold.
   a. defaulted b. deluded c. traversed d. squandered

8. After the salesman lost his job, he ______ on his car loan.
   a. decreed b. averted c. defaulted d. converted

9. The prosecutor told the jury to disregard the defendant's testimony because it was ______ and misleading.
   a. universal b. blissful c. versatile d. deceptive

10. The farmer hired a lawyer to resolve the ______ over the adjoining fields.
    a. adversary b. controversy c. diversion d. consequence

PART B

Circle the letter of the word that is most nearly *opposite* in meaning.

1. adversary
   a. traitor b. planner c. fool d. friend

2. discreet
   a. first b. imprudent c. pleasant d. successful

Name ______________________ Date ______________ Class ______________

Vocabulary Power *continued*

3. **depleted**
   a. filled b. squandered c. converted d. averted

4. **dehydrated**
   a. clever b. sleepy c. silly d. wet

5. **denounce**
   a. remember b. forget c. praise d. throw

PART C

Circle the letter of the word or phrase that means most nearly the same as the vocabulary word.

1. **deceptive**
   a. odd b. misleading c. distribute d. honest

2. **stationary**
   a. moving b. paper c. secretary d. motionless

3. **vain**
   a. leaving b. uncertain c. conceited d. selfless

4. **delude**
   a. welcome b. groan c. rain d. trick

5. **versatile**
   a. multifaceted b. growing c. concern d. one-track

Name ______________________ Date ______________ Class ________

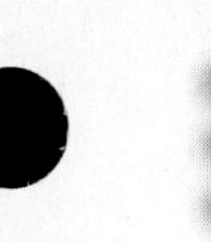

Vocabulary Power

Lesson 18 Using Synonyms

Most people like to play games and, even more, to *win* games. How do you feel when you play a game? Do you have the will to win? The following words have to do with winning, losing, and playing.

Word List

attain	**despondent**	**industrious**	**relinquish**
avid	**euphoric**	**potential**	**vanquish**
contend	**gambol**		

EXERCISE A Synonyms

Each boldfaced vocabulary word is paired with a synonym whose meaning you probably know. Think of other related words and write them on the line provided. Then, look up the vocabulary word in a dictionary and write its meaning.

1. **attain** : acquire ______________________

   Dictionary definition ______________________

2. **avid** : enthusiastic ______________________

   Dictionary definition ______________________

3. **contend** : compete ______________________

   Dictionary definition ______________________

4. **despondent** : discouraged ______________________

   Dictionary definition ______________________

5. **euphoric** : joyful ______________________

   Dictionary definition ______________________

6. **gambol** : play ______________________

   Dictionary definition ______________________

7. **industrious** : hardworking ______________________

   Dictionary definition ______________________

8. **potential** : possible ______________________

   Dictionary definition ______________________

Vocabulary Power *continued*

9. **relinquish** : release ________________________

   Dictionary definition ________________________

10. **vanquish** : conquer ________________________

    Dictionary definition ________________________

EXERCISE B Word Clues

Write the vocabulary word that best matches the clue.

1. A sports fan who never misses a game can be called this. ______________
2. A word that describes the hardworking worker bees. ______________
3. A word that describes a team that has just lost the championship. ______________
4. A word that describes a team that has just won the championship. ______________
5. Lambs skipping in the meadow do this. ______________

EXERCISE C Usage

If the boldfaced word is used correctly in the sentence, write *correct* above it. If not, draw a line through the word and write the correct vocabulary word above it.

1. The only way she could **attain** her college education was by working to earn tuition money.
2. Holding the remote control tightly in her hands, the little girl refused to **gambol** control of it.
3. The army had come to **vanquish** the enemy and return home victorious.
4. Rising at 4:30 every morning, the **potential** golfer drove to the golf course and played at least one round.
5. After getting a sizable raise, the woman was relieved that she did not have to **contend** with money problems anymore.

EXERCISE D Word Illustrations

Think about how the vocabulary words in this lesson relate to winning and losing, both on and off the playing field. On a separate sheet of paper, draw a picture that illustrates the meaning of one or two of the words. Then, write a caption for your drawing, using the word(s) you chose.

Name ______________________ Date ______________ Class 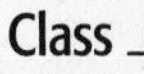 __________

Vocabulary Power

Lesson 19 Sentence Completion

Have you ever dreamed of climbing Mount Everest, rafting down the Colorado River, going on an African safari, or camping out in the wilds of Alaska? If you said yes to any of these questions, you probably have at least some spirit of adventure in you. All the words in the following list have to do with adventure.

Word List

barren	**confrontation**	**flounder**	**immense**
capsize	**endure**	**gratify**	**perilous**
catastrophe	**fate**		

EXERCISE A Sentence Completion

Fill in each blank with the word that best fits from the list. Double-check your answers by looking for the meanings of these words in a dictionary.

1. Dodging bullets and land mines, the soldier made the ______________ journey back to the bunker.
2. The champion weightlifter had ______________ shoulders, arms, and legs.
3. To ______________ their parents, the children cleaned their rooms and started dinner.
4. After a chance meeting with her future husband at the drugstore, the woman always believed that ______________ had brought them together.
5. The businessman did not think he could ______________ another minute of the boring meeting.
6. With no signs of plant or animal life, this part of the desert was ______________ and desolate.
7. As the storm grew worse, the ship's captain realized that the ship was going to ______________, throwing all of his men into the churning water.
8. After the skier lost her balance, she started to ______________ about, trying to stand upright.
9. The unsafe nuclear power plant was a(n) ______________ waiting to happen.
10. After the first day of the trial, upset family members from both sides had an emotional ______________ outside the courthouse.

Vocabulary Power *continued*

EXERCISE B Multiple-Meaning Words

The word *fate* has a variety of meanings. Determine which definition best fits each sentence. In the space to the left, write the number of that definition. Then, on a separate sheet of paper, write a sentence of your own for each definition you chose.

> **fate** *n.* **1.** the power that controls what is to happen, without being able to be controlled by anyone or anything; destiny **2.** one's fortune or lot in life; what happens to someone **3.** what becomes of someone or something **4.** disaster or ruin; death *cap./plural.* **5.** in mythology, the three goddesses–Clotho, Lachesis, and Atropos–who determine the course of human life

______ 1. After the operation, the doctor said whether the patient lived or died now was up to **fate**.

______ 2. According to mythology, the three **Fates** worked together to determine the outcome of a person's life: Clotho spun the thread of life, Lachesis measured and guided it, and Atropos cut the thread to the end of life.

______ 3. The jury took seriously its job of deciding the **fate** of the young man on trial for arson.

______ 4. After her house burned down, the woman wondered why she didn't deserve a better **fate**.

EXERCISE C Synonyms

For each group of words and phrases, write the vocabulary word that best fits.

1. dangerous, risky, hazardous ______________
2. huge, enormous, vast ______________
3. meeting, challenge, argument ______________
4. stumble, struggle, trip ______________
5. please, delight, satisfy ______________
6. outlast, survive, persist ______________

EXERCISE D Sentence Completion

On a separate sheet of paper, write sentences in which you use each of the words in the list correctly. The sentences should show that you understand each word's meaning.

Name ______________________ Date ______________ Class ______________

Vocabulary Power

Lesson 20 The Latin Root *pendere*

The root part of a word carries the word's main meaning. The vocabulary words in this lesson are based on the roots *pend, pens,* and *pond,* which come from the Latin word *pendere*, which means "to weigh" or "to hang."

Word List

compensation	**indispensable**	**poise**	**ponderous**
dependent	**penchant**	**ponder**	**suspend**
expend	**pensive**		

EXERCISE A Synonyms

Each boldfaced vocabulary word is paired with a synonym whose meaning you probably know. Think of other related words and write them on the line provided. Then, look up the vocabulary word in a dictionary and write its meaning.

1. **compensation** : payment ______________________

   Dictionary definition ______________________

2. **dependent** : relying on ______________________

   Dictionary definition ______________________

3. **expend** : use ______________________

   Dictionary definition ______________________

4. **indispensable** : necessary ______________________

   Dictionary definition ______________________

5. **penchant** : liking ______________________

   Dictionary definition ______________________

6. **pensive** : thinking ______________________

   Dictionary definition ______________________

7. **poise** : balance ______________________

   Dictionary definition ______________________

8. **ponder** : think ______________________

   Dictionary definition ______________________

Vocabulary Power continued

9. **ponderous** : heavy ____

____

10. **suspend** : discontinue ____

____

EXERCISE B Synonyms

For each group of words and phrases, write the vocabulary word that best fits.

1. use up, disburse, exhaust ______________
2. serious, reflective, pondering ______________
3. weighty, awkward, massive ______________
4. stop, interrupt, postpone ______________

EXERCISE C Usage

If the boldfaced word is used correctly in the sentence, write *correct* above it. If not, draw a line through the word and write the correct vocabulary word above it.

1. The painters demanded **poise** for the work they had done all week on the apartment buildings.
2. The college student paused for a moment to **ponder** the essay question in the final exam.
3. The drill sergeant told his men not to **expend** all of their energy in the first few miles of the hike.
4. In the lifeboat, the survivors kept things that were **pensive** and threw overboard anything they did not need for survival.
5. The woman with the sweet tooth had a **potential** for chocolate-covered cherries.

EXERCISE D Word Puzzle

For each word or phrase, write in the vocabulary word that best fits. Then, unscramble the circled letters to solve the riddle. The answer is also a vocabulary word.

1. Something paid. ___ ___ ___ (___) (___) ___ (___) ___ ___ (___) ___ ___
2. Another way to say "weighs a lot." ___ ___ (___) ___ (___) ___ ___ ___ (___)
3. An elephant has this for peanuts. ___ ___ (___) ___ ___ (___) ___ ___

A man wears these to keep his pants up.

I ___ D ___ ___ ___ ___ ___ ___ ___ ___ B L ___ suspenders.

Name ______________________ Date ______________ Class ____________

Vocabulary Power

Lesson 21 Using Reading Skills

Understanding Homographs

A homograph is a word that has the same spelling as another word, but a different meaning and word origin. For example, the word *pen* is a homograph, because it means both "a writing instrument" and "a closed yard for sheep or other animals."

Sometimes, a homograph may have two different pronunciations as well. For example, when the word *bow* rhymes with *toe,* it refers to a weapon for shooting arrows. When it rhymes with *cow,* it can refer to the act of bending one's body in greeting or respect or to the forward part of a ship.

When you encounter a homograph in your reading, how do you determine which is the correct meaning? First, you should study the context–the sentence and surrounding sentences in which the word appears. The context will provide you with clues as to the word's meaning, as in the example below.

The singer had a deep, *bass* voice that echoed through the huge marble church.

If you think that *bass* refers to a fish, then the sentence is most likely confusing. However, when you understand that *bass* also means "the lowest male voice in music," then the sentence makes sense. When you check *bass* in the dictionary, you will also discover different pronunciations for the different meanings.

EXERCISE

Study the definition for each word listed below. Then, circle the letter of the sentence with the same meaning.

1. **mail:** armor used for protecting the body against arrows.
   a. The letter carrier delivered **mail** for hours.
   b. Knights wore **mail** in the fifteenth century.

2. **pop:** popular
   a. The cork made a loud **pop** as the bottle was opened.
   b. **Pop** music appeals to many people.

3. **card:** a tool with teeth, such as a wire brush used to clean and straighten wool.
   a. The woman used a **card** to work the wool.
   b. The player couldn't decide which **card** to play.

4. **box:** to pack in a box
   a. Mrs. Allen decided to **box** the cookies and send them to her son.
   b. The champion fighter did not want to **box** anymore.

5. **sty:** a small swelling on the edge of the eyelid
   a. The pigs wallowed in their **sty**.
   b. The **sty** hurt every time she blinked.

Name ______________________ Date ______________ Class ________

Vocabulary Power

Review: Unit 5

EXERCISE

Circle the letter of the word that best completes each sentence.

1. Having a _______ for candy, the little boy stopped to stare at all the varieties in the display case.
   a. penchant b. fate c. gambol d. compensation

2. The ambitious politician wanted to _______ the presidency.
   a. gambol b. poise c. attain d. capsize

3. The crowd was _______ when the home team defeated its biggest rival.
   a. despondent b. barren c. euphoric d. indispensable

4. The _______ high school student worked a part-time job, made the honor roll, and played on the school's volleyball team.
   a. industrious b. ponderous c. dependent d. perilous

5. The Pacific Ocean is a(n) _______ body of water.
   a. pensive b. immense c. barren d. avid

6. The earthquake was the biggest natural _______ of the last decade.
   a. poise b. potential c. catastrophe d. penchant

7. The long-distance runner collapsed a mile before the finish line, having _______ all of her energy.
   a. expended b. endured c. gratified d. vanquished

8. Suffering from a migraine, the pilot _______ control of the plane to his copilot.
   a. floundered b. pondered c. suspended d. relinquished

9. A(n) _______ defender of the environment, the clean-air advocate urged the crowd to join him in his efforts.
   a. dependent b. avid c. perilous d. pensive

10. A _______ occurred between the strikers and those who crossed the picket line.
    a. confrontation b. compensation c. fate d. potential

Name ______________________ Date ______________ Class ________

Vocabulary Power

TEST: Unit 5

PART A

Circle the letter of the word that best completes each sentence.

1. The farmer struggled to eke a living from the ______ land.
   a. avid b. ponderous c. industrious d. barren

2. After waiting months for payment, the technician finally demanded ______ from the computer's owner.
   a. compensation b. confrontation c. poise d. potential

3. In wartime, soldiers and their loved ones must ______ the anguish of separation.
   a. flounder b. capsize c. contend d. endure

4. The lambs ______ in the field on a warm summer day.
   a. suspended b. attained c. gamboled d. expended

5. Pitched overboard in the storm, the man ______ helplessly in the frigid seawater.
   a. floundered b. poised c. pondered d. gratified

6. The terminally ill patient was ______ on his family for support.
   a. pensive b. dependent c. potential d. barren

7. The poet grew increasingly ______ as he received rejection after rejection for his work.
   a. despondent b. ponderous c. euphoric d. avid

8. After weeks of fighting, the weary but determined soldiers finally ______ their adversaries.
   a. relinquished b. pondered c. contended d. vanquished

9. After their chance meeting, the happy couple believed that ______ had brought them together.
   a. confrontation b. catastrophe c. fate d. poise

10. Although she needed much practice, the coach felt that the young athlete had enormous ______.
    a. potential b. compensation c. penchant d. confrontation

Name ______________________ Date ____________ Class ____________

PART B

Circle the letter of the word that is most nearly *opposite* in meaning.

1. **perilous**
   a. dirty b. generous c. safe d. wild

2. **industrious**
   a. likable b. lazy c. sweet d. empty

3. **gratify**
   a. lose b. displease c. include d. frown

4. **ponderous**
   a. thoughtless b. disloyal c. attractive d. light

5. **immense**
   a. tiny b. intelligent c. peaceful d. angry

PART C

Circle the word in parentheses that best completes each sentence.

1. A strong liking is a (poise, penchant, confrontation).
2. To be thoughtful, especially in a sad way, is to be (pensive, perilous, euphoric).
3. Self-assurance and an ease of manner constitute (fate, penchant, poise).
4. To accomplish or to achieve is to (endure, attain, contend).
5. To give up or to release is to (gambol, flounder, relinquish).
6. To spend or to use up is to (expend, attain, vanquish).
7. A great or sudden disaster or misfortune is a (catastrophe, compensation, penchant).
8. To exclude or to cause to stop is to (suspend, gratify, capsize).
9. Absolutely necessary or required is (ponderous, despondent, indispensable).
10. To consider carefully or to think deeply about is to (expend, ponder, vanquish).

Name ______________________ Date ______________ Class ____________

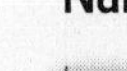

Vocabulary Power

Lesson 22 Using Synonyms

Have you ever had a difficult experience? What was it like? What words would you use to describe it? The words below deal with hard times. You might be able to use some of these words to help you share with others your own experiences with hard times.

Word List

agony	**devastate**	**petrify**	**vulnerable**
bondage	**futile**	**relentless**	**yield**
chagrin	**perish**		

EXERCISE A Synonyms

Each boldfaced word is paired with a synonym whose meaning you probably know. Think of other words related to the synonym and write them on the line provided. Then, look up the vocabulary word in a dictionary and write its meaning.

1. **agony** : suffering ______________________

   Dictionary definition ______________________

2. **bondage** : slavery ______________________

   Dictionary definition ______________________

3. **chagrin** : embarrassment ______________________

   Dictionary definition ______________________

4. **devastate** : destroy ______________________

   Dictionary definition ______________________

5. **futile** : ineffective ______________________

   Dictionary definition ______________________

6. **perish** : die ______________________

   Dictionary definition ______________________

7. **petrify** : frighten ______________________

   Dictionary definition ______________________

8. **relentless** : constant ______________________

   Dictionary definition ______________________

Vocabulary Power *continued*

9. **vulnerable** : weak ____________________

   Dictionary definition ____________________

10. **yield** : submit ____________________

    Dictionary definition ____________________

EXERCISE B Multiple-Meanings Words

The word *yield* has a variety of meanings. Study the meanings listed below. Determine which definition best fits each sentence. To the left, write the number of the definition.

> **yield** *v.* **1.** to produce; to bear **2.** to surrender **3.** to give way under physical force, such as bending **4.** to give way under pressure or influence; to submit to urging or persuasion **5.** to give something in return, such as a profit from an investment. **6.** to grant; to give *n.* **7.** amount that is produced; product

______ 1. The last opposing juror **yielded** and voted "guilty."

______ 2. The mine owner hoped the mine would **yield** enough coal to repay the bank.

______ 3. The stage **yielded** under the weight of hundreds of concert fans.

______ 4. Knowing that the battle could not be won, the general **yielded** to the enemy.

______ 5. In the middle of a severe drought, the farmer was reluctant to predict his crop **yield**.

EXERCISE C Sentence Completion

Fill in the blank with the vocabulary word that best completes each sentence.

1. Knowing that the Latin word *petra* means "stone" should help you understand the meaning of the word ________________.

2. The word ________________ is based on the Latin infinitive *lentare,* which means "to bend," the suffix *-less,* meaning "not," and the prefix *re-,* which means "again."

3. Knowing that the Latin word *devastare* means "to lay waste" should help you understand the meaning of the verb ________________.

4. The word ________________ is based on the French *chagrin,* which means "to become gloomy."

Name ______________________ Date ______________ Class ____________

Vocabulary Power

Lesson 23 Usage

Different people have different ideas of what constitutes a good life. For some, a good life involves wealth; for others, fame. For still others, it might mean enjoying good health and good friends. The words in the list below might help you explain what a good life means to you.

Word List

adapt	**destiny**	**indulge**	**prestigious**
affable	**ecstatic**	**invigorate**	**prosper**
affluence	**felicity**		

EXERCISE A Synonyms

Each boldfaced word is paired with a synonym whose meaning you probably know. Think of other related words and write them on the line provided. Then, look up the vocabulary word in a dictionary and write its meaning.

1. **adapt** : adjust ______________________

   Dictionary definition ______________________

2. **affable** : pleasant ______________________

   Dictionary definition ______________________

3. **affluence** : wealth ______________________

   Dictionary definition ______________________

4. **destiny** : fate ______________________

   Dictionary definition ______________________

5. **ecstatic** : joyful ______________________

   Dictionary definition ______________________

6. **felicity** : happiness ______________________

   Dictionary definition ______________________

7. **indulge** : pamper ______________________

   Dictionary definition ______________________

8. **invigorate** : refresh ______________________

   Dictionary definition ______________________

Vocabulary Power *continued*

9. **prestigious** : famous ______________________________

   Dictionary definition ______________________________

10. **prosper** : succeed ______________________________

   Dictionary definition ______________________________

EXERCISE B Antonyms

Write the vocabulary word that is most nearly *opposite* in meaning.

1. poverty ______________
2. unknown ______________
3. fail ______________
4. depressed ______________
5. sadness ______________

EXERCISE C Usage

If the boldfaced word is used correctly, write *correct* above it. If not, draw a line through the word and write the correct vocabulary word above it.

1. After moving from the country to the city, the family tried to **prosper** to a very different way of life.
2. The teenage boy believed it was his **affluence** to become a world-famous musician.
3. With the house to herself, the tired mother decided to **adapt** herself and take a hot bubble bath.
4. The poor couple became **ecstatic** when they heard they had won the lottery.
5. Skilled in the social graces, the **affable** host made everyone feel at ease.

EXERCISE D Synonyms

For each group of words, write the vocabulary word that best fits.

1. sociable, courteous, polite ______________
2. energize, strengthen, restore ______________
3. riches, abundance, profusion ______________
4. flourish, produce, thrive ______________
5. joy, bliss, delight ______________

EXERCISE E Good News

On a separate sheet of paper, write a letter to a friend in which you describe some good times that you remember, are enjoying now, or look forward to. Use all of the words in the list in your letter and show that you know the meaning of each.

Name ______________________ Date ______________ Class ______________

Vocabulary Power

Lesson 24 The Prefix *dis-*

The prefix of a word serves to change the meaning of the main part of the word. The prefix *dis-* has several meanings. *Dis-* can mean "away" or "apart," "deprive of" or "remove from," "cause to be the opposite of," "fail" or "stop," and "do the opposite of." The words in this list all have the prefix *dis-*.

Word List

discharge	**disgrace**	**distasteful**	**distort**
disclose	**dispatch**	**distinguished**	**distress**
disdainful	**disregard**		

EXERCISE A Synonyms

Each boldfaced word is paired with a synonym whose meaning you probably know. Think of other words related to the synonym and write them on the line provided. Then, look up the vocabulary word in a dictionary and write its meaning.

1. **discharge** : release ______________________

   Dictionary definition ______________________

2. **disclose** : reveal ______________________

   Dictionary definition ______________________

3. **disdainful** : scornful ______________________

   Dictionary definition ______________________

4. **disgrace** : shame ______________________

   Dictionary definition ______________________

5. **dispatch** : send ______________________

   Dictionary definition ______________________

6. **disregard** : ignore ______________________

   Dictionary definition ______________________

7. **distasteful** : unpleasant ______________________

   Dictionary definition ______________________

8. **distinguished** : famous ______________________

   Dictionary definition ______________________

Name ______________________ Date ______________ Class ____________

9. **distort** : twist ______________________________

Dictionary definition ______________________________

10. **distress** : trouble ______________________________

Dictionary definition ______________________________

EXERCISE B Multiple-Meaning Words

Several of the words in this list have more than one meaning. Fill in the blanks with the words that best complete the sentences. To the left, write the number of the definition that helped you make your choice.

> **dispatch** *v.* **1.** to send off or away with speed for a specific purpose, especially for official business **2.** to kill **3.** to get done promptly or quickly; settle *n.* **4.** the sending off of something, as a letter, messenger, and so on **5.** putting to death **6.** a written message or other communication, such as news item or government business. **7.** promptness in doing something; speed.
> **disclose** *v.* **1.** to open up to view; uncover **2.** to reveal or make known.

______ 1. The admiral sent a ______________ to the White House about the terrorist attack.

______ 2. The lion ____________(ed) of the buffalo after a short chase.

______ 3. The psychologist told the police that she could not ______________ confidential information about her patient.

______ 4. The real estate agent opened the door to ______________ a huge walk-in closet.

______ 5. The nurses and doctors in the emergency room worked with ______________ and care.

EXERCISE C Word Association

For each group of words, write the vocabulary word that best fits.

1. overlook, neglect, forget ______________
2. proud, haughty, arrogant ______________
3. worry, agonize, annoy ______________
4. eject, expel, free ______________
5. disagreeable, offensive, hateful ______________

Name ______________________ Date ______________ Class ____________

Vocabulary Power

Lesson 25 The Latin Words *bene* and *mal*

The Latin word *bene* means "well" and *bonus* means "good." The Latin word *mal* means "bad." The words in the following list are based on either the Latin word for "good" or "well," or the Latin word for "bad."

Word List

benefactor	**bountiful**	**malevolent**	**malignant**
benefit	**maladroit**	**malfunction**	**malpractice**
benign	**malady**		

EXERCISE A Sentence Completion

Fill in each blank with the word from the list that best fits. Double-check your answers by looking up the meanings of these words in a dictionary.

1. The woman was heartbroken to learn that her father had a ________________ brain tumor.
2. The ________________ grandfather always had a kind smile and a piece of candy for his grandchildren.
3. The farmers celebrated the ________________ harvest.
4. When his dog died during a routine operation, the child wanted to sue the veterinarian for ________________.
5. After being fired from her job, the ________________ woman planned to get revenge on her former coworkers.
6. The neighborhood raised money to ________________ the family who had lost their house and belongings in a fire.
7. The doctor examined a patient who was suffering from a mysterious ________________.
8. The mechanic told the car owner that he needed to replace the brakes immediately or they would ________________.
9. The successful businessman was a ________________ of the homeless, providing them with food and shelter.
10. The ________________ boy was always tripping and dropping things.

Vocabulary Power *continued*

EXERCISE B Multiple-Meaning Words

Determine which of the words below best completes each sentence. To the left, write the number of the definition that helped you make your choice.

> **benefit** *n.* **1.** something that is for the good of a person or thing; advantage **2.** an event that serves to raise money for a person or cause **3.** Often, **benefits,** *pl.,* a payment or service provided by a pension, health insurance company, or employer *v.* **4.** to be useful or helpful to; to be good for **5.** to receive good; profit
> **benign** *adj.* **1.** gracious; kindly in feeling; having a gentle disposition **2.** showing kindness and gentleness **3.** favorable **4.** mild, as a climate **5.** not threatening to life or health; not malignant

______ **1.** The community held a ______________ to raise money to help fight heart disease.

______ **2.** The candy store owner knew that she would ______________ from the new elementary school that opened across the street.

______ **3.** The patient was relieved to hear that the tumor was ______________.

______ **4.** The kindergartners wanted the ______________ Mrs. Alvarez as their teacher.

______ **5.** The ______________ climate of the Caribbean attracts tourists.

EXERCISE C Synonyms

For each group of words, write the vocabulary word that best fits.

1. clumsy, awkward, inept ______________
2. sickness, ailment, disease ______________
3. abundant, plentiful, overflowing ______________
4. helper, donator, contributor ______________
5. kindly, mild, gracious ______________

EXERCISE D Context Clues

Write the vocabulary word that best matches the clue.

1. Doctors are sometimes sued for this. ______________
2. This is a synonym for showing ill will or hatred. ______________
3. When machines don't work right, they do this. ______________
4. Tuberculosis and the flu are each a kind of this. ______________
5. Something that is harmful in nature can be called this. ______________

Name ______________________ Date ______________ Class ______________

Vocabulary Power

Lesson 26 Using Idiomatic Skills

Understanding Idioms

If your friend told you she was getting "cold feet" about playing volleyball on the school team, you would tell her that getting cold feet is normal and that she would most likely feel more comfortable when she had played a few games. *To get cold feet* means "to become fearful." The idiomatic meaning of the expression is different from its literal meaning. The literal meaning of the phrase *cold feet* is "feet that are cold."

To understand the meaning of an idiom, think about its literal meaning and study its context. Look at the example below.

Dad *went through the roof* when he heard that I got a detention.

Because the context–the fact that the speaker got a detention–tells you that the father would most likely react unfavorably, you can deduce the meaning of the idiom. (*Went through the roof* means "reacted angrily.")

EXERCISE A

Write an expression that could be substituted for each idiom below.

1. His plans to watch a movie with friends *fell through* when he got called back to work. ______________
2. The angry employee *bit his tongue* when his boss criticized his work. ______________
3. Even though the teenager was thin, he could still *eat like a horse*. ______________
4. No one confided in Beatrice because she was *loose lipped.* ______________
5. The grandfather said he was getting too *long in the tooth* to be jogging. ______________

EXERCISE B

To the left, write the letter and number of the idiom that best completes each sentence.

straighten up 1. stand something upright. **2.** clean up. **3.** improve behavior. **4.** stand straighter. **put down 1.** bring to an end; stop. **2.** degrade; belittle; criticize. **3.** put into writing. **4.** land an airplane.

______ 1. The military leader decided to ______________ the uprising before it got out of control.

______ 2. Thomas's parents told him he had to ______________ his room before lunch.

______ 3. The manager warned the employee to ______________ or lose his job.

______ 4. Mr. Shim told his daughter that it was not nice to ______________ other people.

______ 5. The voice teacher was always telling her slouching singers to ______________.

Name ______________________ Date ______________ Class ______________

Vocabulary Power

Review: Unit 6

EXERCISE

Circle the letter of the word that best completes each sentence.

1. The shipwrecked passengers sent out a _______ signal.
   a. felicity b. bondage c. distress d. discharge

2. The hurricane _______ houses for a mile along the coast.
   a. devastated b. disgraced c. benefited d. distinguished

3. The doctor thought it was too early to _______ the patient from the hospital.
   a. malpractice b. discharge c. invigorate d. distort

4. The dieter decided to _______ in one small scoop of ice cream.
   a. adapt b. yield c. prosper d. indulge

5. Upon learning that the girl was lost, the police _______ a team to search the woods behind her house.
   a. disgraced b. dispatched c. benefited d. disregarded

6. Fifty-five million people _______ during World War II.
   a. petrified b. perished c. distorted d. malfunctioned

7. After identifying the patient's serious _______, the doctor admitted her to the hospital immediately.
   a. malady b. bondage c. affluence d. chagrin

8. After training for ten years, the gymnast was _______ to hear that he made the U.S. Olympic team.
   a. relentless b. vulnerable c. distasteful d. ecstatic

9. Even after she fell ill, the _______ old woman still had a smile and a kind word for everyone.
   a. benign b. malevolent c. malignant d. disdainful

10. The judge told the man convicted of drunk driving that he was a _______ to his family.
    a. dispatch b. disgrace c. benefit d. discharge

Name ______________________ Date ______________ Class ____________

Vocabulary Power

Test: Unit 6

PART A

Circle the letter of the word that is most nearly *opposite* in meaning.

1. **bountiful**
   a. unattractive b. stingy c. depressed d. dark

2. **futile**
   a. cold b. calm c. effective d. considerate

3. **felicity**
   a. sadness b. danger c. warmth d. intelligence

4. **distasteful**
   a. happy b. clean c. agreeable d. pleasant

5. **ecstatic**
   a. loose b. clear c. strong d. unhappy

PART B

Circle the letter of the word that best completes the sentence.

1. The office manager returned the copy machine because it ______ several times a day.
   a. malfunctioned b. yielded c. prospered d. distinguished

2. Ever since she was young, the woman thought that it was her ______ to become a celebrated author.
   a. chagrin b. affluence c. destiny d. malady

3. After hours of ______ questioning by the military, the prisoner finally broke down and signed the confession.
   a. ecstatic b. bountiful c. relentless d. benign

4. After permanently injuring his back, the soldier was ______ from the army.
   a. benefited b. adapted c. perished d. discharged

5. Family members often comfort each other in times of ______.
   a. dispatch b. distress c. affluence d. felicity

6. The newspaper reporter refused to ______ the name of her source.
   a. disclose b. petrify c. invigorate d. malfunction

7. Upon winning the ______ award, the previously unknown author found himself in the national spotlight.
   a. malpractice b. affable c. prestigious d. maladroit

8. Some slaves escaped from ______ through the Underground Railroad.
   a. affluence b. bondage c. malady d. disregard

9. As a reward for losing weight, the woman ______ herself by buying a new outfit.
   a. disgraced b. distorted c. adapted d. indulged

10. The doctor told the patient that, although the tumor was ______, it had not spread to other parts of the body.
    a. disdainful b. malignant c. vulnerable d. futile

PART C

Circle the word in parentheses that best completes each sentence.

1. A(n) (disdainful, futile, affable) person is likely to be welcomed as a team member.
2. If you (petrify, yield, distort) the truth, you twist it.
3. A(n) (ecstatic, prestigious, maladroit) person is unlikely to choose ballet as a career.
4. People might tend to fear you if you have a (benign, disdainful, distinguished) smile.
5. An out-of-control car can (disgrace, distress, invigorate) pedestrians.

Name ______________________ Date ______________ Class ____________

Vocabulary Power

Lesson 27 Using Synonyms

Have you heard any good stories lately? What do you think makes a story good? The characters? The plot? The style of the storyteller? The words in the following list have to do with stories and storytelling.

Word List

captivate	**dauntless**	**legendary**	**proclaim**
champion	**dispute**	**majestic**	**quest**
climax	**lament**		

EXERCISE A Synonyms

Each boldfaced word is paired with a synonym whose meaning you probably know. Think of other words related to the synonym and write them on the line provided. Then, look up the vocabulary word in a dictionary and write its meaning.

1. **captivate** : fascinate ______________________

   Dictionary definition ______________________

2. **champion** : support ______________________

   Dictionary definition ______________________

3. **climax** : summit ______________________

   Dictionary definition ______________________

4. **dauntless** : brave ______________________

   Dictionary definition ______________________

5. **dispute** : argument ______________________

   Dictionary definition ______________________

6. **lament** : mourn ______________________

   Dictionary definition ______________________

7. **legendary** : famous ______________________

   Dictionary definition ______________________

8. **majestic** : magnificent ______________________

   Dictionary definition ______________________

Name ______________________ Date ______________ Class ____________

Vocabulary Power *continued*

9. **proclaim** : declare ______________________

 Dictionary definition ______________________

10. **quest** : adventure ______________________

 Dictionary definition ______________________

EXERCISE B Multiple-Meaning Words

Fill in the blanks with the words that best complete the sentences. To the left, write the number of the definition that fits.

> **champion** *n.* **1.** winner of first place in a game or contest **2.** person who fights for another person or cause; supporter *v.* **3.** to fight for; to defend; to support
> **lament** *v.* **1.** to mourn aloud for; to wail **2.** to express sorrow or to mourn for **3.** to regret *n.* **4.** a crying out in grief; a wail **5.** a poem or song that expresses grief

______ **1.** When his brother died suddenly, the poet composed a ______ to be read at the funeral.

______ **2.** George won the final round to become chess ______ of his school district.

______ **3.** With four dogs and two cats of his own, Sal was an active ______ of animal rights.

______ **4.** The citizens came to the memorial to ______ their beloved mayor's death.

______ **5.** The senator believed she had been elected to ______ the cause of the poor.

EXERCISE C Synonyms

For each group of words write the vocabulary word that best fits.

1. search, journey, pursuit ______________
2. well-known, mythical, fabulous ______________
3. grand, noble, glorious ______________
4. argue, discuss, debate ______________
5. attract, charm, delight ______________

EXERCISE D Sentence Construction

On a separate sheet of paper, write sentences in which you use each of the words in the list correctly. The sentences should show that you understand each word's meaning.

Name ______________________ Date ______________ Class ____________

Vocabulary Power

Lesson 28 The Prefixes *over-* and *under-*

As you know, the word *over* means "above" and the word *under* means "beneath." These words also appear in other words as prefixes. The prefix of a word serves to change the meaning of the main part of the word. The words in the following list have either *over-* or *under-* as prefixes.

Word List

overbearing	**oversight**	**underhanded**	**undermine**
overcast	**overture**	**underling**	**underscore**
overcome	**undergo**		

EXERCISE A Synonyms

Each boldfaced word is paired with a synonym whose meaning you probably know. Think of other words related to the synonym and write them on the line provided. Then, look up the vocabulary word in a dictionary and write its meaning.

1. **overbearing** : dominating ______________________

   Dictionary definition ______________________

2. **overcast** : gloomy ______________________

   Dictionary definition ______________________

3. **overcome** : conquer ______________________

   Dictionary definition ______________________

4. **oversight** : instance of forgetting ______________________

   Dictionary definition ______________________

5. **overture** : offer ______________________

   Dictionary definition ______________________

6. **undergo** : endure ______________________

   Dictionary definition ______________________

7. **underhanded** : sly ______________________

   Dictionary definition ______________________

8. **underling** : inferior ______________________

   Dictionary definition ______________________

Vocabulary Power *continued*

9. **undermine** : weaken ______________________________

   Dictionary definition ______________________________

10. **underscore** : emphasize ______________________________

   Dictionary definition ______________________________

EXERCISE B Multiple-Meaning Words

Fill in the blanks with the words that best complete the sentences. To the left, write the number of the definition that fits.

> **oversight** *n.* **1.** watchful and capable care **2.** failure to notice or remember something
> **overture** *n.* **1.** proposal; offer **2.** the music played by an orchestra as an introduction to a dramatic musical work
> **underscore** *v.* **1.** to draw a line under **2.** to emphasize; to stress *n.* **3.** a line drawn under text, especially to emphasize or to indicate use of italics **4.** music that accompanies a movie's action and dialogue

______ **1.** The police officer ________________(d) the importance of staying away from strangers.

______ **2.** The director apologized to the cast for the ________________ on the program.

______ **3.** The university hospital made a(n) ________________ to the country's leading cancer specialist to join its staff.

______ **4.** The composer wrote an energetic, lively ________________ for the adventure movie.

______ **5.** The television news anchor ________________(d) the words that she wanted to emphasize.

EXERCISE C Usage

If the boldfaced word is used correctly in the sentence, write *correct* above it. If it is not, draw a line through the word and write the correct vocabulary word above it.

1. To win the last stronghold, the colonel planned to **underscore** the enemy.
2. Tired of being an **overture** to so many bosses, the woman applied for a job in management.
3. The bride and groom were disappointed by the **overcast** sky on their wedding day.
4. The cancer patient refused to **underscore** more treatment.
5. Known for his **underhanded** ways, the worker was not trusted by his fellow workers.

Name ______________________ Date ______________ Class ____________

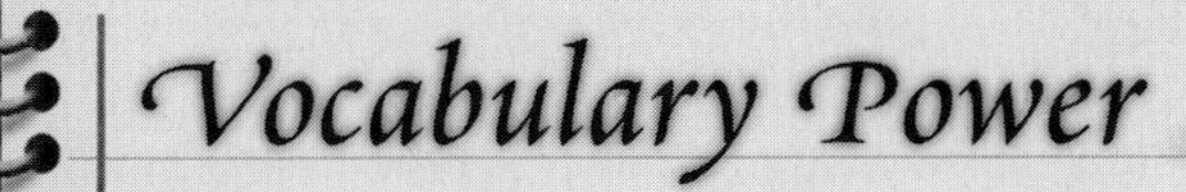

Lesson 29 The Prefix *re-*

A prefix serves to change the meaning of the main part of the word. The prefix *re-* has two main meanings: "back" and "again." The words in the following list have *re-* as a prefix.

Word List

recede	**refined**	**renounce**	**repulsive**
reconciliation	**refuge**	**replenish**	**retain**
reconnaissance	**remorseful**		

EXERCISE A Synonyms

Each boldfaced word is paired with a synonym whose meaning you probably know. Think of other words related to the synonym and write them on the line provided. Then, look up the vocabulary word in a dictionary and write its meaning.

1. **recede** : withdraw ______________________

   Dictionary definition ______________________

2. **reconciliation** : agreement ______________________

   Dictionary definition ______________________

3. **reconnaissance** : military survey ______________________

   Dictionary definition ______________________

4. **refined** : well-mannered ______________________

   Dictionary definition ______________________

5. **refuge** : shelter ______________________

   Dictionary definition ______________________

6. **remorseful** : regretful ______________________

   Dictionary definition ______________________

7. **renounce** : resign ______________________

   Dictionary definition ______________________

8. **replenish** : fill ______________________

   Dictionary definition ______________________

Name ______________________ Date ______________ Class ____________

Vocabulary Power continued

9. **repulsive** : disgusting ______________________

   Dictionary definition ______________________

10. **retain** : keep ______________________

   Dictionary definition ______________________

EXERCISE B Etymology

Following are the Latin words and their meanings that are the basis of some of the vocabulary words. The prefix *re-*, which usually means either "back" or "again," comes before each word. Write the vocabulary word related to each Latin word and definition. Then, write another word that might also be based on each Latin word. Double-check your answers by looking up the words in a dictionary. If you cannot think of another word, use a dictionary to find one; then, note its meaning.

1. *re-* plus *cedere*, which means "to move back" ______________
2. *re-* plus *plenus*, which means "full" ______________
3. *re-* plus *fugere*, which means "to flee" ______________
4. *re-* plus *nuntiare*, which means "to announce" ______________
5. *re-* plus *concilium*, which means "bond of union" ______________

EXERCISE C Synonyms

For each group of words, write the vocabulary word that best fits.

1. sorrowful, contrite, regretful ______________
2. revolting, offensive, obnoxious ______________
3. examination, exploration ______________
4. settlement, harmony, accord ______________
5. polite, educated, respectful ______________

EXERCISE D Sentence Construction

On a separate sheet of paper, write sentences in which you use the words on the list correctly. The sentences should show that you understand each word's meaning.

Name ______________________ Date ______________ Class ____________

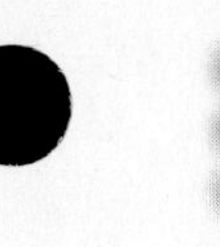

Vocabulary Power

Lesson 30 The Latin Root *ven*

The root part of a word carries the word's main meaning. The vocabulary words in this lesson are based on the root *ven,* which comes from the Latin word *venire,* meaning "to come."

Word List

circumvent	**conventional**	**revenue**	**venture**
convene	**intervene**	**uneventful**	**venue**
convenient	**inventory**		

EXERCISE A Synonyms

Each boldfaced word is paired with a synonym whose meaning you probably know. Think of other words related to the synonym and write them on the line provided. Then, look up the vocabulary word in a dictionary and write its meaning.

1. **circumvent** : outwit ______________________

   Dictionary definition ______________________

2. **convene** : meet ______________________

   Dictionary definition ______________________

3. **convenient** : handy ______________________

   Dictionary definition ______________________

4. **conventional** : customary ______________________

   Dictionary definition ______________________

5. **intervene** : interfere ______________________

   Dictionary definition ______________________

6. **inventory** : list ______________________

   Dictionary definition ______________________

7. **revenue** : income ______________________

   Dictionary definition ______________________

8. **uneventful** : peaceful ______________________

   Dictionary definition ______________________

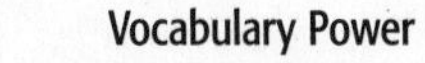

Name ______________________ Date ______________ Class ____________

Vocabulary Power *continued*

9. **venture** : dare ______________________

Dictionary definition ______________________

10. **venue** : place ______________________

Dictionary definition ______________________

EXERCISE B Multiple-Meaning Words

Fill in the blanks with the words that best complete the sentences. To the left, write the number of the definition that fits.

convene *v.* **1.** to meet for a purpose; to gather together **2.** to call together (members of a group, etc.)
venture *v.* **1.** to expose to risk or danger **2.** to take on the risk or dangers of; to brave **3.** to dare when rejection or embarrassment might result **4.** to dare to say or make (a comment) *n.* **5.** a daring or risky endeavor **6.** something, such as money or property, at risk in a speculative venture
venue *n.* **1.** the place or area of a crime or cause of action **2.** the place where a jury is summoned and a trial held

______ **1.** The hotel manager decided to ______________ the hotel staff to present the new health insurance policy.

______ **2.** Because of the sensational publicity, the lawyer tried to change the ______________ for her client's trial.

______ **3.** After their parents had disciplined them, none of the children ______________(d) a comment about the punishment.

______ **4.** Teachers ______________ every August to plan for the upcoming school year.

______ **5.** The acrobats ______________ onto the tight rope every performance.

EXERCISE C Usage

If the boldfaced word is used correctly in the sentence, write *correct* above it. If it is not, draw a line through the word and write the correct vocabulary word above it.

1. The landlord received **venture** from the three houses he rented out.
2. The moviegoer **circumvented** the long lines by buying tickets over the phone earlier in the day.
3. The police were called to **intervene** in a clash between strikers and nonstrikers.
4. The bus stopped in front of the businesswoman's apartment, making it **uneventful** for her.
5. Once a week, the manager studied his **venue** to determine what items he needed to restock.

Name ______________________ Date ______________ Class ______________

Vocabulary Power

Lesson 31 Using Reading Skills

Using Dictionary Respellings

People use dictionaries to look up the meanings and pronunciations of unfamiliar words. Dictionaries provide respellings that indicate pronunciation. Respellings use special symbols that tell how to pronounce letters. For example, a dictionary respelling of the word *sight* would look like this: *sīt*

The following chart lists some respelling symbols, their corresponding sounds, and some words in which they appear.

For Long Vowel Sounds, a straight line over the vowel is used.

ā	mate
ē	wheel
ī	mine
ō	bone
ū	tune

For Short Vowel Sounds, the letter appears with no symbol.

a	hat
e	pet
i	sit
o	odd
u	under

Other Vowel Sounds

ä	father
ər	turn
ô	cough
oi	boy
oo	food
ou	hour
yü	view

Some Consonant Sounds

hw	wheat
th	thick
th (underlined)	that
zh	division

In addition to showing the sounds in words, respellings also indicate accent. The accent symbo') appears next to the syllable that is to be stressed. For example, for the word *extreme,* the ac it is on the second syllable, as shown in this respelling: *ek strēm'*.

EXERCISE A

Study the respellings below. Use the pronunciation guide to answer t' questions.

1. *distaste* (dis tāst') Does the second syllable rhyme with *paste* or *pa* ______________

2. *azure* (azh'ər) Does the *z* sound like the *z* in *lazy* or the *s* in *sure*? ______________

3. *douse* (dous) Does the word rhyme with *boss* or *blou* ______________

EXERCISE B

Use the chart above to write the dictionary respelling for each word below. For more respelling symbols, consult the front of the dictionary.

1. hire ______________ 3. wheat ______________

2. ruler ______________ 4. sprout ______________

Name ______________________________ Date ______________ Class __________

Vocabulary Power

Review: Unit 7

EXERCISE A

Circle the letter of the word that best completes each sentence.

1. The aging grandmother had to _______ three heart surgeries in less than two years.
   a. captivate b. undergo c. proclaim d. recede

2. Three days of heavy rain helped to _______ the dangerously low water supply.
   a. replenish b. lament c. champion d. undermine

3. At the garage sale, two customers who wanted the same item had an angry _______ over it.
   a. reconciliation b. venture c. dispute d. overcast

4. The _______ thief asked for mercy before the judge pronounced the sentence.
   a. dauntless b. refused c. majestic d. remorseful

5. The fast food manager studied the _______ to decide what food he needed to reorder.
   a. oversight b. inventory c. venue d. reconnaissance

6. The mother witnessed the tearful _______ between her sons.
   a. venture b. refuge c. reconnaissance d. reconciliation

7. The flight was _______ after the storm had passed.
   a. uneventful b. convenient c. repulsive d. remorseful

8. The teachers asked the principal to _______ in the dispute.
   a. recede b. intervene c. renounce d. retain

9. The sky was _______ with threatening clouds.
   a. overbearing b. underhanded c. overcast d. conventional

10. The popular player received an attractive _______ from the competition.
   a. underscore b. inventory c. refuge d. overture

EXERCISE B **Antonyms**

Circle the word that is the *opposite of* the boldfaced word.

1. **underling**	subordinate	leader	follower
2. **convene**	disperse	meet	assemble
3. **refined**	pure	cultivated	impure
4. **overcome**	surmount	surrender	vanquish
5. **overbearing**	dominant	overpowering	subservient

Name ______________________ Date ______________ Class __________

Vocabulary Power

Test: Unit 7

PART A

Write the letter of the word that best completes the sentence.

1. After not speaking for two years, the brothers had a tearful ______ at their sister's wedding.
   a. underling b. inventory c. dispute d. reconciliation

2. After two days with no rain, the flood waters finally began to ______.
   a. venture b. lament c. recede d. underscore

3. The folk heroes Paul Bunyan, Johnny Appleseed, and Davy Crockett were all ______ figures.
   a. legendary b. convenient c. overcast d. repulsive

4. Many early explorers were on a(n) ______ to find gold and other riches.
   a. overture b. revenue c. quest d. champion

5. Threatened by an uprising, the king ______ his throne and fled the country.
   a. renounced b. intervened c. championed d. refined

6. The president's cabinet members ______ at the White House to discuss the crisis.
   a. underwent b. convened c. replenished d. retained

7. At the company's monthly staff meeting, no one ______ to ask the owner a question about the raises that were promised.
   a. circumvented b. captivated c. disputed d. ventured

8. Instead of wearing the ______ white wedding gown, the bride decided to wear a black pantsuit.
   a. repulsive b. underhanded c. conventional d. remorseful

9. Caught in a thunderstorm, the joggers sought ______ in an abandoned farmhouse.
   a. refuge b. revenue c. climax d. reconnaissance

10. The sprinter ______ many hardships to realize her dream of running on the Olympic track team.
    a. proclaimed b. retained c. underscored d. overcame

PART B

Choose the letter of the word that is most nearly *opposite* in meaning.

1. overcast
   a. warm b. humid c. sunny d. delicious

Vocabulary Power continued

2. **majestic**
   a. lowly b. stingy c. wrong d. angry

3. **overbearing**
   a. tasteful b. simple c. attractive d. humble

4. **undermine**
   a. strengthen b. please c. soothe d. love

5. **repulsive**
   a. shy b. attractive c. generous d. slow

PART C

Circle the letter of the best answer.

1. A person of lower rank or position can be described as ______.
   a. a champion b. an underling c. an oversight d. a refuge

2. **Revenue** means ______.
   a. an examination of funds
   b. a high point or summit
   c. income or money coming in
   d. an oversight

3. "Handy," "easy to use," and "within easy reach" are all ways to define ______.
   a. convenient b. remorseful c. legendary d. underhanded

4. A synonym for **dauntless** is ______.
   a. legendary b. majestic c. overbearing d. fearless

5. The most exciting part of a story is its ______.
   a. venture b. inventory c. climax d. oversight

Name ______________________ Date ______________ Class ______________

Vocabulary Power

Lesson 32 Using Synonyms

Did you ever prepare for a journey to a place you had never been before? How did you feel? What did you expect to happen when you got there? What were the people like? The landscape? The words in the following list relate to journeys to unfamiliar places.

Word List

antagonist	**encroach**	**hail**	**outlandish**
cosmopolitan	**enterprising**	**novel**	**trepidation**
disquieting	**excursion**		

EXERCISE A Synonyms

Each boldfaced vocabulary word is paired with a synonym whose meaning you probably know. Think of other words related to the synonym and write them on the line provided. Then, look up the vocabulary word in a dictionary and write its meaning.

1. **antagonist** : enemy ______________________

   Dictionary definition ______________________

2. **cosmopolitan** : worldly ______________________

   Dictionary definition ______________________

3. **disquieting** : disturbing ______________________

   Dictionary definition ______________________

4. **encroach** : intrude ______________________

   Dictionary definition ______________________

5. **enterprising** : resourceful ______________________

   Dictionary definition ______________________

6. **excursion** : trip ______________________

   Dictionary definition ______________________

7. **hail** : greet ______________________

   Dictionary definition ______________________

8. **novel** : new ______________________

   Dictionary definition ______________________

9. **outlandish** : strange ______________________

   Dictionary definition ______________________

Name ______________________ Date ______________ Class ______________

Vocabulary Power *continued*

10. **trepidation** : fear ______________________

Dictionary definition ______________________

EXERCISE B Multiple-Meaning Words

Fill in the blanks with the words below that best complete the sentences. To the left, write the number of the definition you use.

> **hail** *n.* **1.** precipitation in the form of small, round pieces of ice **2.** a shower that resembles hail **3.** a shout of welcome; a greeting **4.** a loud shout to attract attention *v.* **5.** to precipitate hail **6.** to pour down like hail **7.** to salute or greet **8.** to signal to or call out **9.** to greet with approval or acclaim
> **novel** *adj.* **1.** of a new kind, nature, etc.; new; unfamiliar; strange *n.* **2.** a written story with characters and a plot, long enough to fill at least one volume

_______ 1. People ran for cover as ______________ bounced against the ground.

_______ 2. The parents ran out of the house to ______________ their son who had just arrived home from the army.

_______ 3. The writer's goal was to write one ______________ a year.

_______ 4. The inventor came up with a ______________ idea for baking bread faster.

_______ 5. When the piñata broke, the children found themselves under a ______________ of candy.

EXERCISE C Synonyms

For each group of words and phrases, write the vocabulary word that best fits.

1. opponent, foe, rival ______________
2. sophisticated, international ______________
3. journey, voyage, expedition ______________
4. odd, bizarre, peculiar ______________

EXERCISE D Word Illustrations

Think about how the vocabulary words in this list relate to taking a trip to an unfamiliar place. On a separate sheet of paper, draw a picture that illustrates the meaning of one or two of the words. Then, write a caption for your drawing, using the words.

Name ______________________ Date ______________ Class ______________

Vocabulary Power

Lesson 33 The Latin Roots *specere* and *species*

The root part of a word carries the word's main meaning. Some of the roots of the vocabulary words in this lesson are based on the Latin word *specere,* which means "to look." Others are based on the Latin word *species,* which means "a kind."

Word List

aspect	**despicable**	**specimen**	**speculate**
circumspect	**prospect**	**specter**	**suspect**
conspicuous	**specify**		

EXERCISE A Synonyms

Each boldfaced word is paired with a synonym whose meaning you probably know. Think of other words related to the synonym and write them on the line provided. Then, look up the vocabulary word in a dictionary and write its meaning.

1. **aspect** : appearance ______________________

   Dictionary definition ______________________

2. **circumspect** : cautious ______________________

   Dictionary definition ______________________

3. **conspicuous** : noticeable ______________________

   Dictionary definition ______________________

4. **despicable** : contemptible ______________________

   Dictionary definition ______________________

5. **prospect** : expectation ______________________

   Dictionary definition ______________________

6. **specify** : name ______________________

   Dictionary definition ______________________

7. **specimen** : sample ______________________

   Dictionary definition ______________________

8. **specter** : spirit ______________________

   Dictionary definition ______________________

Name ______________________ Date ______________ Class ____________

9. **speculate** : think ______________________

Dictionary definition ______________________

10. **suspect** : doubt ______________________

Dictionary definition ______________________

EXERCISE B Multiple-Meaning Words

Fill in the blank with the words below that best complete the sentences. To the left, write the number of the definition that fits.

prospect *n.* **1.** something that is looked forward to or expected **2.** expectation; the act of looking forward to or expecting **3.** person thought to become a candidate, customer, etc. **4.** scene; view *v.* **5.** to explore an area for gold, oil, etc.
suspect *v.* **1.** to imagine to exist or be true **2.** to imagine (one) to be guilty with little or no evidence **3.** to distrust; to feel no confidence in *n.* **4.** person who is regarded with suspicion; one who is suspected

_______ **1.** In 1848, thousands rushed to San Francisco to ______________ for gold.

_______ **2.** The main ______________ in the bank robbery was a career thief.

_______ **3.** The ______________ of a vacation was attractive to the couple who had been working overtime for months.

_______ **4.** The police officer ____________(ed) that this was not the first time the man had driven under the influence of alcohol.

_______ **5.** The presidential ______________ withdrew because of insufficient funds.

EXERCISE C Synonyms

For each group of words, write the vocabulary word that best fits.

1. mention, name, designate ______________
2. visible, obvious, prominent ______________
3. ponder, consider, reason ______________
4. sample, illustration, instance ______________
5. ghost, apparition, phantom ______________

Name ______________________ Date ______________ Class ______________

Vocabulary Power

Lesson 34 The Latin Root *tempus* and the Greek Root *chronos*

The root part of a word carries the word's main meaning. Some of the roots of the vocabulary words in this lesson are based on the Latin word *tempus,* which means "time." Others are based on the Greek word *chronos,* which also means "time."

Word List

chronic	**contemporary**	**temperamental**	**tempest**
chronicle	**synchronize**	**temperance**	**tempo**
chronological	**temper**		

EXERCISE A Synonyms

Each boldfaced word is paired with a synonym whose meaning you probably know. Think of other words related to the synonym and write them on the line provided. Then, look up the vocabulary word in a dictionary and write its meaning.

1. **chronic** : constant ______________________

   Dictionary definition ______________________

2. **chronicle** : record ______________________

   Dictionary definition ______________________

3. **chronological** : ordered ______________________

   Dictionary definition ______________________

4. **contemporary** : modern ______________________

   Dictionary definition ______________________

5. **synchronize** : coincide ______________________

   Dictionary definition ______________________

6. **temper** : soften ______________________

   Dictionary definition ______________________

7. **temperamental** : unpredictable ______________________

   Dictionary definition ______________________

8. **temperance** : restraint ______________________

   Dictionary definition ______________________

Name ______________________ Date ______________ Class ____________

9. **tempest** : storm ______________________

   Dictionary definition ______________________

10. **tempo** : pace ______________________

   Dictionary definition ______________________

EXERCISE B **Multiple-Meaning Words**

Fill in the blanks with the words below that best complete the sentences. Some words may appear in the plural form in the sentences. To the left, write the number of the definition that fits.

chronic *adj.* **1.** lasting a long time or recurring frequently **2.** suffering from a disease that is chronic **3.** never stopping; habitual; constant
contemporary *adj.* **1.** living in the same time period **2.** of the same age or date **3.** of or having to do with the present time; modern *n.* **4.** person living in the same time period as others
temperance *n.* **1.** moderation in speech, thought, habits, etc.; restraint; self-control **2.** being moderate in the drinking of alcoholic beverages

______ 1. Walt Whitman was a ______________ of Abraham Lincoln.

______ 2. Asthma is a ______________ disease.

______ 3. Martha's coworkers avoided her because she was a ______________ complainer.

______ 4. In 1920, ______________ societies helped enact Prohibition, which made the manufacture, transportation, and sale of alcoholic beverages illegal.

______ 5. She furnished her home in ______________ style.

EXERCISE C **Usage**

If the boldfaced word is used correctly in the sentence, write *correct* above it. If not, draw a line through the word and write the correct vocabulary word above it.

1. The writer decided to **chronicle** the life of his father, an emigrant from Europe.
2. After playing a slow song, the band decided to pick up the **temper.**
3. A time line is arranged in **chronic** order.
4. The line dancers worked together to **synchronize** their movements.
5. With the **temperance** upon them, the crew struggled to keep the ship afloat.

Name ________________ Date ________ Class ________

Vocabulary Power

Lesson 35 Using Reading Skills

Using Base Words

The main part of a word is its root, which carries the central meaning. For example, the root of *immaturely* is *mature*, from the Latin *maturus,* meaning "ripe." If the root is a complete word, it is called a base word. To determine the base, simply take away any prefix or suffix. A prefix precedes the base word; a suffix follows. Both change the word's meaning. The prefix in *immaturely* is *im-,* which means "not." The suffix *–ly*, meaning "how," creates an adverb of manner. When you remove the prefix and suffix, you are left with the base word *mature.*

EXERCISE

For each of the words below, underline the base word and write its definition. Then, write another word formed from the same base word.

1. unbreakable ________________

2. disabled ________________

3. unreliable ________________

4. distrustful ________________

5. unclassified ________________

6. immobile ________________

7. mishandled ________________

8. unbearable ________________

9. dishonesty ________________

10. untainted ________________

Name ______________________ Date ______________ Class ______________

Vocabulary Power

Review: Unit 8

EXERCISE

Circle the letter of the word that best completes each sentence.

1. After smoking for thirty years, the man had a(n) ______ cough.
   a. enterprising b. chronic c. chronological d. cosmopolitan

2. After seeing the ______ movie, the man found it difficult to sleep.
   a. contemporary b. conspicuous c. disquieting d. circumspect

3. The judge called stealing money from a woman in a wheelchair a ______ crime.
   a. despicable b. novel c. temperamental d. conspicuous

4. The family went on a short ______ to a nearby state park.
   a. specter b. hail c. excursion d. antagonist

5. The doctor did not want to ______ about the patient's health until the blood tests came back.
   a. synchronize b. encroach c. chronicle d. speculate

6. The critic had to ______ his reactions to the violent film.
   a. temper b. specify c. hail d. synchronize

7. Without a(n) ______, Daniel had no reason to continue debating the question.
   a. novel b. chronicle c. specter d. antagonist

8. Sally felt ______ in her Parisian gown.
   a. suspect b. conspicuous c. despicable d. chronic

9. Scrooge was haunted by the ______ of Christmas Past.
   a. trepidation b. tempest c. specter d. excursion

10. Wendy decided to put her writing portfolio in ______ order.
    a. chronological b. outlandish c. contemporary d. novel

Name _______________ Date _______________ Class _______________

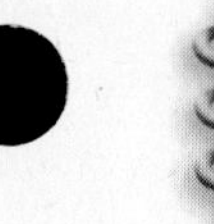

Vocabulary Power

Test: Unit 8

PART A

Circle the letter of the word that best completes the sentence.

1. After watching the freshmen work out, the coach thought that there was only one good ______ for his baseball team.
   a. tempo b. antagonist c. prospect d. tempest

2. The biographer has put the events of the poet's life in ______ order, from her birth to her death.
   a. chronological b. conspicuous c. contemporary d. disquieting

3. The ______ young woman used her invention to create her own company.
   a. despicable b. enterprising c. chronic d. circumspect

4. Realizing he might hurt his daughter's feelings, the father tried to ______ his harsh words with a smile and a pat on the back.
   a. temper b. speculate c. hail d. encroach

5. The owners did not want strangers to pet their ______ dog because he was sometimes unpredictable.
   a. cosmopolitan b. novel c. outlandish d. temperamental

6. Upon leaving the theater, the couple ______ a taxicab to take them to their apartment.
   a. suspected b. chronicled c. hailed d. encroached

7. Caught in the middle of the ______, the captain struggled against the wind and rain.
   a. tempest b. tempo c. excursion d. specimen

8. After months of fighting, the general finally surrendered to his ______.
   a. antagonist b. aspect c. specter d. suspect

9. The marching band teacher taught his students how to march together and ______ their movements.
   a. encroach b. speculate c. specify d. synchronize

10. Before 1920, groups that supported ______ worked to outlaw the sale of alcohol.
    a. specimen b. temperance c. chronicle d. temper

Vocabulary Power continued

PART B

Circle the letter of the word that is most nearly *opposite* in meaning.

1. conspicuous
   a. hidden b. calm c. clean d. familiar

2. novel
   a. pretty b. disturbing c. ordinary d. hard

3. contemporary
   a. proud b. old-fashioned c. serious d. late

4. disquieting
   a. loud b. nervous c. comforting d. intelligent

5. circumspect
   a. overweight b. critical c. imprudent d. adventurous

PART C

Choose the letter of the vocabulary word that best matches the clue.

1. This kind of person feels at home in all areas of the world. _______
   a. contemporary b. conspicuous c. cosmopolitan d. novel

2. If you want to record the history of your village or town, you would write this. _______
   a. chronicle b. tempest c. antagonist d. contemporary

3. Clues as to a person's guilt would cause you to do this. _______
   a. hail him or her c. prospect him or her
   b. synchronize him or her d. suspect him or her

4. If someone dresses in an unusual or a bizarre way, you might describe the person's appearance in this way. _______
   a. cosmopolitan b. outlandish c. circumspect d. enterprising

5. A person who practices moderation in action and conduct is said to have this virtue or quality. _______
   a. trepidation b. temperance c. excursion d. prospect

abide ə bīd′
adapt ə dapt′
adversary ad′vər ser′ē
affable af′ə bəl
affluence af′lo͞o əns
agony ag′ə nē
alarm ə lärm′
amass ə mas′
amphibious am fib′ē əs
animated an′ə mā′tid
anthropology an′thrə pol′ə jē
antibiotic an′tē bī ot′ik
anticipation an tis′ə pā′shən
apiary ā′pē er′ē
aptitude ap′tə to͞od′
aquatic ə kwat′ik
arboreal är bôr′ē əl
aspect as′pekt
attain ə tān′
aversion ə vur′zhən
avert ə vurt′
avid av′id
barren bar′ən
benefactor ben′ə fak′tər
benefit ben′ə fit
benign bi nīn′
bewilderment bi wil′dər mənt
biology bī ol′ə jē
blissful blis′fəl
bondage bon′dij
botany bot′ən ē
bountiful boun′ti fəl
box boks
burrow bur′ō
camouflage kam′ə fläzh′
capsize kap′sīz
captivate kap′tə vāt′
card kärd
carnivorous kär niv′ər əs
catastrophe kə tas′trə fē′
chagrin shə grin′
champion cham′pē ən
chronic kron′ik
chronicle kron′i kəl
chronological kron′ə loj′i kəl
circumscribe sur′kəm skrīb′
circumspect sur′kəm spekt′
circumvent sur′kəm vent′
climax klī′maks
commotion kə mō′shən
communal kə mūn′əl
compassion kəm pash′ən
compensation kom′pən sā′shən
confrontation kon′frun tā′shən
conquest kon′kwest
conscription kən skrip′shən
consequence kon′sə kwens′
conspicuous kən spik′ū əs
contemporary kən tem′pə rer′ē
contend kən tend′
controversy kon′trə vur′sē
convene kən vēn′
convenient kən vēn′yənt
conventional kən ven′shən əl
convert kən vurt′
cope kōp
copious kō′pē əs
cosmopolitan koz′mə pol′ə tən
cultivate kul′tə vāt′
cunning kun′ing
cymbal sim′bəl
dauntless dônt′lis
deception di sep′shən
deceptive di sep′tiv
deduce di do͞os′
default di fôlt′
defective di fek′tiv
defiance di fī′əns
dehydrated dē hī′drāt id
dejection di jek′shən
delinquent di ling′kwənt
delude di lo͞od′
demote di mōt′
denounce di nouns′
dependent di pen′dənt
depleted di plē′ tid
designate dez′ig nāt′
despicable des′pi kə bəl
despondent di spon′dənt
destiny des′tə nē

devastate dev′əs tāt′
died dīd
disable dis ā′bəl
discharge dis chärj′
disclose dis klōz′
discreet dis krēt′
disdainful dis dān′fəl
disgrace dis grās′
dishonesty dis on′is tē
dispatch dis pach′
dispute dis pūt′
disquieting dis kwī′i ting
disregard dis′ri gärd′
distasteful dis tāst′fəl
distinguished dis ting′gwisht
distort dis tôrt′
distress dis tres′
distrustful dis trust′fəl
diversion di vur′zhən
dwell dwel
dyed dīd
ecstatic ek stat′ik
edifice ed′ə fis
embroider em broi′dər
emphasize em′fə sīz′
emphatic em fat′ik
employ em ploi′
enable i nā′bəl
encounter en koun′tər
encroach en krōch′
endeavor en dev′ər
endorse en dôrs′
endure en door′
engaging en gā′jing
enterprising en′tər prī′zing
envelop en vəl′əp
euphoric ū fôr′ik
excursion iks kur′zhən
expend iks pend′
extroverted eks′trə vur′tid
fate fāt
felicity fi lis′ə tē
feline fē′līn
flounder floun′dər
forlorn fôr lôrn′
futile fū′til
gait gāt
gambol gam′bəl
genes jēnz
gilt gilt
gratify grat′ə fī′
habitat hab′ə tat′
hail hāl
haughty hô′tē
heal hēl
heed hēd
hoard hôrd
hole hōl
homicide hom′ə sīd′
homogeneous hō′mə jē′nē əs
hostile host′əl
hover huv′ər
humane hū mān′
immense i mens′
immobile i mō′bil
immobilize i mō′bə līz′
impudent im′pyə dənt
indispensable in′dis pen′sə bəl
indulge in dulj′
industrious in dus′trē əs
inscription in skrip′shən
insignia in sig′nē ə
intervene in′tər vēn′
intrigue n. in′trēg, v. in trēg′
inventory in′vən tôr′ē
invigorate in vig′ə rāt′
jargon jär′gən
jeans jēnz
kindred kin′drid
lair lār
lament lə ment′
laughingstock laf′ing stok′
legendary lej′ən der′ē
limelight līm′līt′
luminous lōō′mə nəs
lure loor
lurk lurk
mail māl
majestic mə jes′tik
maladroit mal′ə droit′

malady mal′ ə dē
malevolent mə lev′ ə lənt
malfunction mal′fungk′shən
malignant mə lig′ nənt
malpractice mal prak′ tis
maul môl
meager mē′ gər
mighty mī′ tē
mingle ming′ gəl
misery miz′ ər ē
mishandled mis hand′ əld
missed mist
mist mist
mobile mō′ bəl
momentary mō′ mən ter′ ē
momentous mō men′ təs
momentum mō men′ təm
morning môr′ ning
mortified môr′ tə fīd
motive mō′ tiv
mourning môr′ ning
nondescript non′di skript′
novel nov′ əl
nurture nur′ chər
original ə rij′ ən əl
outlandish out lan′ dish
overbearing ō′ vər bār′ ing
overcast ō′ vər kast′
overcome ō′ vər kum′
oversight ō′ vər sīt′
overture ō′ vər choor′
pang pang
parish par′ ish
peak pēk
peek pēk
penchant pen′ chənt
pensive pen′ siv
perilous per′ ə ləs
perish per′ ish
petrify pet′ re fī′
philanthropy fi lan′ thrə pē
playful plā′ fəl
poise poiz
ponder pon′ dər
ponderous pon′ dər əs
pop pop
potential pə ten′ shəl
prestigious pres tēzh′ əs
principle prin′ sə pəl
procession prə sesh′ ən
proclaim prə klām′
promote prə mōt′
prospect pros′ pekt
prosper pros′ pər
quest kwest
reap rēp
recede ri sēd′
reconciliation rek′ ən sil′ ē ā′ shən
reconnaissance ri kon′ ə səns
recover ri kuv′ ər
redeemed ri dēmd′
refined ri fīnd′
reflective ri flek′ tiv
refuge ref′ ūj
relentless ri lent′ lis
reliance ri lī′ əns
relinquish ri ling′ kwish
remorseful ri môrs′ fəl
remote ri mōt′
renounce ri nouns′
replenish ri plen′ ish
repulsive ri pul′ siv
resent ri zent′
resident rez′ ə dənt
resigned ri zīnd′
retain ri tān′
retreat ri trēt′
revenue rev′ ə nōō′
sentiment sen′ tə mənt
shuffle shuf′ əl
significant sig nif′ i kənt
sincere sin sēr′
solace sol′ is
solitude sol′ ə tōōd′
specify spes′ ə fī′
specimen spes′ ə mən
specter spek′ tər
speculate spek′ yə lāt′
squabble skwob′ əl
squander skwon′ dər

stairs stārz
stares stārz
stationary stā′shə ner′ē
sty stī
subscribe səb skrīb′
sulk sulk
superb soo purb′
suspect sə spekt′
suspend sə spend′
synchronize sing′krə nīz′
temper tem′pər
temperamental tem′prə ment′əl
temperance tem′pər əns
tempest tem′pist
tempo tem′pō
terrarium tə rār′ē əm
transcribe tran skrīb′
traverse trav′ərs
treacherous trech′ər əs
trepidation trep′ə dā′shən
unanimous ū nan′ə məs
unbearable un bār′ə bəl
unbreakable un brā′kə bəl
unclassified un′klas′ə fīd
undergo un′dər gō′
underhanded un′dər han′did
underling un′dər ling
undermine un′dər mīn′
underscore un′dər skôr′
uneventful un′i vent′fəl
unique ū nēk′
universal ū′nə vur′səl
unreliable un′ri lī′ə bəl
untainted un tānt′id
urn urn
vain vān
vanquish vang′kwish
venture ven′chər
venue ven′ū
versatile vur′sə til
vicinity vi sin′ə tē
vulnerable vul′nər ə bəl
wade wād
waive wāv
weighed wād
whole hōl
wry rī
yield yēld
zoology zō ol′ə jē

Answer Key

Unit 1

Lesson 1

A. Words listed in order of placement.
unique; anticipation; hostile; alarm; resent; bewilderment; cope; defiance; pang; mortified

B. 1. unique 2. correct 3. hostile
4. correct 5. bewilderment

C. 1. 3; alarm 2. 1; anticipation 3. 2; hostile
4. 2; alarm 5. 2; pang

D. Student sentences will vary.

Lesson 2

A. Sample synonyms and dictionary definitions are provided.
1. Synonyms include to stitch. embroider: to ornament with needlework; embellish.
2. Synonyms include to accentuate. emphasize: to give intensity to a speech sound, stress.
3. Synonyms include assertive. emphatic: expressed forcefully, attracting special attention.
4. Synonyms include to give a job to. employ: to make use of; use, provide with a job that pays wages or a salary.
5. Synonyms include to permit. enable: to provide with the means or opportunity.
6. Synonyms include to confront. encounter: to meet especially by chance, a chance meeting.
7. Synonyms include to attempt. endeavor: to strive, a serious effort.
8. Synonyms include to sign the back of a check, champion. endorse: to approve publicly.
9. Synonyms include attractive. engaging: tending to draw favorable attention.
10. Synonyms include to cover. envelop: to enclose or enfold completely with or as if with a covering.

B. 1. 2; endorse 2. 1; employ 3. 2; employ
4. 3; embroider 5. 1; endorse

C. Student letters will vary.

Lesson 3

A. Sample synonyms and dictionary definitions are provided.
1. Synonyms include to put up with. abide: to wait for, tolerate, endure.
2. Synonyms include joint. communal: shared, owned by members of a community.
3. Synonyms include to abide. dwell: to live as a resident, exist.
4. Synonyms include structure. edifice: building, a large structure.
5. Synonyms include relatives. kindred: a group of related individuals.
6. Synonyms include to cultivate. nurture: to supply with food, educate.
7. Synonyms include trust. reliance: state of having confidence in someone or something.
8. Synonyms include lodger. resident: one who lives in a place.
9. Synonyms include opinion. sentiment: an attitude, thought, or judgment prompted by feeling, an emotion.
10. Synonyms include area. vicinity: a surrounding area or district.

B. 1. kindred 2. reliance 3. communal 4. nurture

C. Related words will vary.
1. resident 2. communal 3. vicinity 4. nurture
5. sentiment 6. reliance 7. edifice

D. Student pictures will vary; captions should include vocabulary words.

Lesson 4

A. Student answers may vary.
1. plain 2. honest 3. candid 4. honorable

B. Answers will vary, but students' words and phrases should be synonyms of the word *mighty.*

Review: Unit 1

1. d 2. a 3. d
4. a 5. c 6. b
7. a 8. c 9. d
10. c

Test: Unit 1

A. 1. b 2. c 3. a
4. d 5. b 6. c
7. d 8. a 9. c
10. c

B. 1. b 2. a 3. d
4. c 5. b 6. d

C. 1. b 2. a 3. d
4. c

Unit 2

Lesson 5

A. Words listed in order of placement in paragraph.
haughty; lair; shuffle; lure; gait; aquatic; cunning; lurk; feline; solitude

B. 1. aquatic 2. lure 3. haughty
4. cunning 5. lurk

C. 1. 2 2. 5 3. 3
4. 1 5. 4

D. 1. correct 2. lair 3. correct
4. gait 5. lure

E. Student pictures will vary; captions should include vocabulary words.

Lesson 6

A. Student answers will vary; sample dictionary definitions are provided.
1. philanthropy: goodwill to others, a gift to promote welfare.
2. anthropology: the study of human beings.
3. biology: a branch of knowledge that deals with living organisms and vital processes.
4. animated: full of movement and activity.
5. homicide: a killing of one human being by another.
6. antibiotic: a substance able to inhibit or kill a microorganism.
7. humane: marked by compassion, sympathy, or consideration for humans or animals.
8. homogeneous: of the same or a similar kind or nature.
9. amphibious: able to live both on land and in water.
10. unanimous: being of one mind, agreeing.

B. 1. anthropology 2. correct 3. animated
4. correct 5. correct 6. correct
7. correct 8. humane

C. 1. biology 2. animated 3. amphibious
Ans. He was hopping mad.

Lesson 7

A. 1. botany; zoology 2. habitat 3. arboreal
4. cultivate; reap 5. burrow; carnivorous 6. terrarium
7. apiary

B. 1. apiary 2. arboreal 3. burrow
4. terrarium 5. reap

C. 1. carnivorous 2. botany 3. habitat 4. arboreal

D. 1. cultivate 2. habitat 3. burrow 4. reap

E. Student sentences will vary.

Lesson 8

A. Sample synonyms and dictionary definitions are provided.
1. Synonyms include turbulence. commotion: confusion, unrest.
2. Synonyms include downgrade. demote: to reduce to a lower grade or rank.
3. Synonyms include to paralyze. immobilize: to prevent freedom of movement.
4. Synonyms include traveling. mobile: adaptable, versatile, characterized by the mixing of social groups.
5. Synonyms include temporary. momentary: having a very brief life.
6. Synonyms include serious. momentous: significant, consequential.
7. Synonyms include incentive. momentum: a property of a moving body that determines the length of time required to bring it to rest when under

the action of a constant force or moment, stimulation.

8. Synonyms include explanation. motive: something that causes a person to act; tending to move to action.
9. Synonyms include to encourage. promote: to advance in station, rank, or honor.
10. Synonyms include isolated. remote: out of the way, secluded, far removed.

B. 1. commotion 2. momentous 3. promote
4. demote 5. mobile 6. immobilize
7. momentary 8. remote

C. 1. 4; remote 2. 1; promote 3. 3; remote
4. 1; remote 5. 2; remote 6. 3; promote
7. 2; promote

D. Student paragraphs will vary but should show that students understand the meaning of the vocabulary words.

Lesson 9

Answers will vary; sample dictionary definitions are provided.

1. circumspect: careful.
2. miserly: stingy.
3. luminous: bright.
4. copious: plentiful.
5. playful: mischievous.
6. relinquish: surrender.

Review: Unit 2

1. b 2. c 3. c 4. a
5. d 6. b 7. a 8. b
9. d 10. c

Test: Unit 2

A. 1. c 2. a 3. c 4. b
5. d 6. d 7. b 8. a
9. c 10. d

B. Student answers will vary; sample answers are provided.

1. No, because *animated* means lively.
2. Yes, because bees can give dangerous stings when handled by an inexperienced person.
3. No, to cultivate friendship requires positive communication.
4. Yes, alligators need a water habitat.
5. No, *unanimous* means "one mind."
6. Yes, your uncle cares for and maintains trees.
7. Yes, *carnivorous* animals subsist on animal flesh.
8. Yes, because *botany* is the science dealing with plants.
9. No, because *commotion* is agitation and disturbance.
10. Yes, because finance requires the management of money and calls for computational skills.

Unit 3

Lesson 10

A. 1. reflective 2. limelight 3. aptitude
4. forlorn 5. superb 6. impudent
7. laughingstock 8. sulk 9. mingle
10. squabble

B. 1. aptitude 2. impudent
3. squabble 4. forlorn

C. 1. sulk 2. limelight 3. laughingstock
4. mingle 5. superb 6. reflective

D. Answers will vary.

Lesson 11

A. 1. procession 2. conquest 3. treacherous
4. retreat 5. meager 6. jargon
7. amass 8. camouflage 9. intrigue
10. hover

B. 1. jargon 2. procession 3. amass
4. correct 5. correct

C. 1. meager 2. amass 3. conquest
4. retreat 5. treacherous

D. 1. 1; hover 2. 3; intrigue 3. 3; hover
4. 1; intrigue 5. 2; hover

E. Sentences will vary.

Lesson 12

A. Sample synonyms and dictionary definitions are provided.

1. Synonyms include to encircle, trace a line around. circumscribe: to define or mark off carefully, to limit.
2. Synonyms include call-up, call of duty. conscription: enrollment of persons for military service.
3. Synonyms include to appoint. designate: to indicate and set apart for a purpose.
4. Synonyms include lettering, dedication. inscription: wording on a coin or medal, dedication of a book.
5. Synonyms include emblem, badge, symbol. insignia: a distinguishing mark or sign.
6. Synonyms include uninteresting, colorless. nondescript: lacking distinctive qualities.
7. Synonyms include willing, agreeable. resigned: to accept something as inevitable.
8. Synonyms include meaningful, notable, vital. significant: having meaning or importance.
9. Synonyms include to promise a gift by signing name. subscribe: to give consent or approval by writing one's name, to order a publication service, to give hearty approval.
10. Synonyms include to write down, record for broadcast. transcribe: to make a written copy of, to record.

B. 1. designate 2. significant 3. insignia
4. nondescript

C. 1. conscription 2. inscription 3. subscribe
4. insignia 5. nondescript

D. 1. circumscribe 2. transcribe 3. designate
Answer: He was resigned.

Lesson 13

Definitions will vary but should be similar in meaning to the following:

1. converted into something of value
2. made up for
3. feel well again
4. get back something taken away; regain
5. first; earliest

Review: Unit 3

1. c 2. b 3. a
4. d 5. b 6. c
7. b 8. a 9. b
10. c

Test: Unit 3

A. 1. b 2. c 3. a
4. d 5. a 6. b
7. c 8. c 9. a
10. c

B. 1. d 2. b 3. d
4. a 5. c

C. 1. c 2. a 3. b
4. b 5. d

Unit 4

Lesson 14

A. Sample synonyms and dictionary definitions are provided.

1. Synonyms include radiant, happy, ecstatic. blissful: marked by contentment.
2. Synonyms include tenderness, kindness, mercy. compassion: pity.
3. Synonyms include outcome, effect, end. consequence: a conclusion derived through logic.
4. Synonyms include false, lying, deceiving. deceptive: misleading.

5. Synonyms include modest, prudent, unobtrusive. discreet: showing good judgment.
6. Synonyms include to listen, pay attention, obey. heed: to notice, to bear in mind.
7. Synonyms include to gather, stash, accumulate. hoard: to amass, to garner.
8. Synonyms include consolation, comfort. solace: deliverance; to relieve.
9. Synonyms include to spend, misuse, throw away. squander: to expend, to drain.
10. Synonyms include useless, foolish, conceited. vain: futile, inadequate, self-glorifying.

B. 1. correct 2. compassion 3. vain
4. heed 5. correct

C. 1. blissful 2. heed 3. squander
4. solace 5. deceptive 6. hoard

Lesson 15

A. Sample synonyms and dictionary definitions are provided.
1. Synonyms include opponent, foe, antagonist. adversary: one that opposes, enemy.
2. Synonyms include loathing, disgust, distaste. aversion: a feeling of dislike for something.
3. Synonyms include to turn away, sidetrack, look away, avoid. avert: to turn away or aside.
4. Synonyms include conflict, disagreement, argument. controversy: discussion marked by expression of opposing views, quarrel.
5. Synonyms include to change, alter, modify. convert: to bring over from one belief to another, to alter the physical or chemical properties.
6. Synonyms include recreation, amusement, sport. diversion: something that amuses or passes time agreeably.
7. Synonyms include friendly, sociable. extroverted: uninhibited, unreserved, gregarious.
8. Synonyms include to go against, oppose. traverse: to act in opposition, travel across or over.
9. Synonyms include common, total, whole. universal: covering all without limit, present everywhere.
10. Synonyms include flexible, pliant. versatile: variable, turning with ease from one thing to another.

B. 1. adversary 2. traverse 3. extroverted
4. avert 5. universal 6. controversy

C. 1. aversion 2. versatile 3. correct
4. traverse 5. correct 6. correct

D. Sentences will vary.

Lesson 16

A. Sample synonyms and dictionary definitions are provided.
1. Synonyms include lie, falsehood. deception: fraud, trickery.
2. Synonyms include to infer, reason. deduce: to arrive at a conclusion from a generalization.
3. Synonyms include to miss, fall short. default: to fail to meet an obligation.
4. Synonyms include parched. dehydrated: having water removed, to lose water.
5. Synonyms include sorrow, grief, depression. dejection: lowness of spirits.
6. Synonyms include cautious, thought out. deliberate: characterized by careful consideration, slow and unhurried.
7. Synonyms include unpaid, someone who breaks the law. delinquent: overdue in payment, violating the law.
8. Synonyms include trick, deceive. delude: to mislead the judgment of another.
9. Synonyms include to blame, to criticize. denounce: to blame publicly.
10. Synonyms include drained, empty. depleted: emptied of.

B. Related words will vary.
1. denounce 2. dehydrated 3. default
4. deduce 5. dejection 6. depleted
7. delude 8. deliberate

C. 1. 1; delinquent 2. 3; deliberate 3. 1; deliberate
4. 2; delinquent

Lesson 17

A. Homophones and definitions will vary.
1. heal: v. to cure or mend.
heel; he'll
2. urn: n. large vase.
earn
3. cymbal: n. a musical instrument made up of one or a pair of brass or bronze plates.
symbol
4. parish: n. a local district of a church.
perish
5. wry: adj. distorted; v. to writhe.
rye
6. principle: n. a general truth or fundamental belief; a rule of ethics or law.
principal
7. stationary: adj. fixed; motionless.
stationery
8. waive: v. to give up (a claim or a right); defer.
wave
9. maul: v. to injure; handle roughly. n. a heavy mallet.
mall
10. gilt: n. a thin layer or coating of gold.
guilt

B. 1. stairs 2. correct 3. mist
4. correct 5. genes 6. dyed
7. correct 8. weighed

Review: Unit 4

1. c 2. b 3. c
4. a 5. d 6. b
7. a 8. c 9. b
10. d

Test: Unit 4

A. 1. b 2. c 3. a
4. b 5. d 6. a
7. c 8. c 9. d
10. b

B. 1. d 2. b 3. a
4. d 5. c

C. 1. b 2. d 3. c
4. d 5. a

Unit 5

Lesson 18

A. Sample synonyms and dictionary definitions are provided.
1. Synonyms include to reach, get, gain. attain: to come by or arrive at.
2. Synonyms include eager. avid: enthusiastic, greedy.
3. Synonyms include to battle, struggle, fight. contend: to strive for in contest.
4. Synonyms include gloomy, depressed. despondent: feeling extreme discouragement.
5. Synonyms include thrilled, excited. euphoric: feeling elated.
6. Synonyms include romp, frolic. gambol: to skip about in play.
7. Synonyms include diligent, busy. industrious: persistently active.
8. Synonyms include likely, probable. potential: possible, something that can develop.
9. Synonyms include to abandon, give up. relinquish: to give up control of.
10. Synonyms include to defeat, overcome. vanquish: to subdue, gain mastery over.

B. 1. avid 2. industrious 3. despondent
4. euphoric 5. gambol

C. 1. correct 2. relinquish 3. correct
4. avid 5. correct

D. Student pictures will vary; captions should include vocabulary words.

Lesson 19

A. 1. perilous 2. immense 3. gratify
4. fate 5. endure 6. barren

7. capsize 8. flounder 9. catastrophe
10. confrontation

B. 1. 1 2. 5 3. 3 4. 2

C. 1. perilous 2. immense 3. confrontation
4. flounder 5. gratify 6. endure

D. Sentences will vary.

Lesson 20

A. Sample synonyms and dictionary definitions are provided.
1. Synonyms include reward, wages, salary. compensation: to make appropriate payment.
2. Synonyms include conditional. dependent: relying on another, subject to another's jurisdiction.
3. Synonyms include to use up, consume. expend: to pay out.
4. Synonyms include essential, vital, needed. indispensable: absolutely necessary.
5. Synonyms include bent, affinity. penchant: a strong inclination, leaning.
6. Synonyms include dreamy, musing. pensive: dreamily thoughtful.
7. Synonyms include confidence, assurance. poise: social confidence.
8. Synonyms include to contemplate, meditate. ponder: to reflect on, think deeply.
9. Synonyms include bulky, weighty. ponderous: unwieldy, clumsy.
10. Synonyms include to defer, hold up. suspend: to set aside.

B. 1. expend 2. pensive 3. ponderous 4. suspend

C. 1. compensation 2. correct 3. correct
4. indispensable 5. penchant

D. 1. compensation 2. ponderous 3. penchant
Answer: indispensable suspenders

Lesson 21

1. b 2. b 3. a
4. a 5. b

Review: Unit 5

1. a 2. c 3. c
4. a 5. b 6. c
7. a 8. d 9. b
10. a

Test: Unit 5

A. 1. d 2. a 3. d
4. c 5. a 6. b
7. a 8. d 9. c
10. a

B. 1. c 2. b 3. b
4. d 5. a

C. 1. penchant 2. pensive 3. poise
4. attain 5. relinquish 6. expend
7. catastrophe 8. suspend 9. indispensable
10. ponder

Unit 6

Lesson 22

A. Sample synonyms and dictionary definitions are provided.
1. Synonyms include anguish, torment. agony: intense pain of mind or body.
2. Synonyms include captivity. bondage: serfdom, servitude to a controlling person or force.
3. Synonyms include disquiet, distress. chagrin: disquietude of mind caused by humiliation, disappointment, or failure.
4. Synonyms include to lay waste, to annihilate. devastate: to bring to ruin or desolation by violent action, to reduce to chaos, disorder, or helplessness.
5. Synonyms include senseless, useless, without rhyme or reason. futile: serving no useful purpose.
6. Synonyms include to depart, to expire, to succumb. perish: to become destroyed or ruined.
7. Synonyms include to harden, to stun. petrify: to make rigid, to confound with fear, amazement, or awe.
8. Synonyms include stern, stubborn. relentless: adamant, showing no abatement of severity, intensity, strength, or pace.
9. Synonyms include susceptible, open. vulnerable: open to attack and damage.
10. Synonyms include to surrender, to give up, to hand over. yield: to give way, give in.

B. 1. 4 2. 1 3. 3
4. 2 5. 7

C. 1. petrify 2. relentless
3. devastate 4. chagrin

Lesson 23

A. Sample synonyms and dictionary definitions are provided.
1. Synonyms include to modify, fit. adapt: to make fit, often by modification.
2. Synonyms include friendly. affable: being pleasant and at ease when talking with others.
3. Synonyms include well-being, prosperity. affluence: wealth, an abundant flow or supply.
4. Synonyms include inevitability, fortune. destiny: a predetermined course of events.
5. Synonyms include experiencing strong emotion. ecstatic: being in a state of overwhelming emotion, especially delight.
6. Synonyms include joy. felicity: the quality or state of being happy.
7. Synonyms include to treat with leniency or generosity. indulge: to gratify someone's desires, to humor, to give free rein to.
8. Synonyms include to stimulate. invigorate: to give life to, to animate.
9. Synonyms include honored, influential. prestigious: holding a commanding position in people's minds.
10. Synonyms include to enjoy good luck or good fortune. prosper: to succeed in an enterprise, to become strong.

B. 1. affluence 2. prestigious 3. prosper
4. ecstatic 5. felicity

C. 1. adapt 2. destiny 3. indulge or invigorate
4. correct 5. correct

D. 1. affable 2. invigorate 3. affluence
4. prosper 5. felicity

E. Student letters will vary but should use all of the vocabulary words correctly.

Lesson 24

A. Sample synonyms and dictionary definitions are provided.
1. Synonyms include to dismiss, to shoot. discharge: to relieve of a burden, to fire off, to unload.
2. Synonyms include to bring to light. disclose: to expose to view.
3. Synonyms include proud, arrogant. disdainful: treating as beneath one's dignity, openly scornful.
4. Synonyms include dishonor, shame. disgrace: loss of favor or honor.
5. Synonyms include to carry out promptly. dispatch: to send off with promptness and speed.
6. Synonyms include to be inattentive, to overlook. disregard: to neglect, to pay no attention to.
7. Synonyms include disagreeable. distasteful: loathsome, offensive to personal taste.
8. Synonyms include well-known for excellence. distinguished: marked by eminence, distinction, or excellence.
9. Synonyms include to contort, to warp. distort: to twist out of proportion, meaning, or shape.
10. Synonyms include discomfort, disquiet, affliction. distress: a painful condition, agony.

B. 1. 6; dispatch 2. 2; dispatch 3. 2; disclose
4. 1; disclose 5. 7; dispatch

C. 1. disregard 2. disdainful 3. distress
4. discharge 5. distasteful

Lesson 25

A. 1. malignant 2. benign 3. bountiful
4. malpractice 5. malevolent 6. benefit

7. malady 8. malfunction 9. benefactor
10. maladroit

B. 1. 2; benefit 2. 5; benefit 3. 5; benign
4. 1 or 2; benign 5. 4; benign

C. 1. maladroit 2. malady 3. bountiful
4. benefactor 5. benign

D. 1. malpractice 2. malevolent 3. malfunction
4. malady 5. malignant

Lesson 26

A. Sample answers follow:
1. were not realized, did not happen
2. stopped himself from saying anything
3. eat a large amount of food
4. had a tendency to talk a lot; lacked the ability to keep a secret
5. old

B. 1. 1; put down 2. 2; straighten up
3. 3; straighten up 4. 2; put down
5. 4; straighten up

Review: Unit 6

1. c 2. a 3. b 4. d
5. b 6. b 7. a 8. d
9. a 10. b

Test: Unit 6

A. 1. b 2. c 3. a 4. c
5. d

B. 1. a 2. c 3. c 4. d
5. b 6. a 7. c 8. b
9. d 10. b

C. 1. affable 2. distort 3. maladroit
4. disdainful 5. distress

Unit 7

Lesson 27

A. Sample synonyms and dictionary definitions are provided.
1. Synonyms include to enchant. captivate: to charm with wit, beauty, or intelligence.
2. Synonyms include to endorse, to stand behind. champion: to fight for, to advocate.
3. Synonyms include the highest point. climax: crest, crown, peak, top.
4. Synonyms include courageous, fearless. dauntless: audacious, bold.
5. Synonyms include a heated discussion, debate. dispute: disagreement, controversy.
6. Synonyms include to grieve; to feel, show, or express grief. lament: to express deep sorrow, to wail.
7. Synonyms include relating to a legend. legendary: well-known.
8. Synonyms include imposing, splendid, grand. majestic: stately and dignified, impressive.
9. Synonyms include to bring to public notice, to announce. proclaim: to praise publicly, to state publicly.
10. Synonyms include a search. quest: a pursuit, an adventurous journey.

B. 1. 5; lament 2. 1; champion 3. 2; champion
4. 2; lament 5. 3; champion

C. 1. quest 2. legendary 3. majestic
4. dispute 5. captivate

D. Sentences will vary.

Lesson 28

A. Sample synonyms and dictionary definitions are provided.
1. Synonyms include overwhelming, high-and-mighty. overbearing: domineering, arrogant, overpowering.
2. Synonyms include cloudy, dull, dim. overcast: clouded over, covered.
3. Synonyms include to win a victory over, to defeat. overcome: to beat, subdue, vanquish.
4. Synonyms include an inadvertent mistake, a slight. oversight: a failure to notice something.
5. Synonyms include an initiative, an introductory action. overture: an orchestral opening, an opening of negotiations, a proposal.
6. Synonyms include to experience, to go through. undergo: to be subjected to, to suffer.
7. Synonyms include deceitful, treacherous, devious. underhanded: deceptive, crafty.
8. Synonyms include one belonging to a lower class. underling: subordinate.
9. Synonyms include to lessen the strength of, to enfeeble. undermine: to weaken by secret means.
10. Synonyms include to accentuate. underscore: to underline, to feature, to accent.

B. 1. 2; underscore 2. 2; oversight 3. 1; overture
4. 2; overture 5. 1; underscore

C. 1. overcome 2. underling 3. correct
4. undergo 5. correct

Lesson 29

A. Sample synonyms and dictionary definitions are provided.
1. Synonyms include to move back or away from a point. recede: to grow less, to diminish.
2. Synonyms include a re-establishment of friendship or harmony. reconciliation: settlement or resolution, agreement.
3. Synonyms include exploration, investigation. reconnaissance: a preliminary survey to gain information.
4. Synonyms include made pure by a commercial process, characterized by discriminating taste. refined: fastidious, cultivated, educated.
5. Synonyms include the state of being safeguarded, an institution that provides care and shelter. refuge: something to which one has recourse in difficulty, protection.
6. Synonyms include feeling or expressing regret for one's misdeeds. remorseful: filled with a gnawing distress for past wrongs, penitent.
7. Synonyms include to give up a possession, claim, or right. renounce: to refuse to obey any further, to give up a right, usually with great sacrifice.
8. Synonyms include to build up, to replace. replenish: to supply fully, to stock, to replace.
9. Synonyms include offensive, extremely unpleasant to the senses or feelings. repulsive: arousing aversion, forbidding, disgusting.
10. Synonyms include to employ, to have, to hold, to remember. retain: to obtain the use or services of, to keep at one's disposal, to have and maintain in one's possession, to renew in the mind.

B. Related words will vary.
1. recede 2. replenish 3. refuge
4. renounce 5. reconciliation

C. 1. remorseful 2. repulsive 3. reconnaissance
4. reconciliation 5. refined

D. Sentences will vary.

Lesson 30

A. Sample synonyms and dictionary definitions are provided.
1. Synonyms include to skirt, to go around. circumvent: to hem in, to make a circuit around, to get around by ingenuity.
2. Synonyms include to call together, to assemble. convene: to summon, to come together in a body.
3. Synonyms include expedient, fit, appropriate, near at hand. convenient: suited to a particular situation.
4. Synonyms include orthodox, conformist, traditional. conventional: lacking originality, ordinary, commonplace.
5. Synonyms include to come between. intervene: to occur or lie between two things.
6. Synonyms include stock, list of goods on hand. inventory: the quantity of goods or materials on hand, an itemized list of assets.
7. Synonyms include income such as taxes collected by a government, gross income. revenue: the total income produced by a given source.
8. Synonyms include not momentous. uneventful: not marked by significant occurrences.

9. Synonyms include to risk, to gamble. venture: to expose to possible hazard, to offer at risk of rejection; a risky act.
10. Synonyms include locale. venue: the place from which a jury is drawn and in which a trial is held, site.

B. 1. 2; convene 2. 2; venue 3. 4; ventured
4. 1; convene 5. 2; venture

C. 1. revenue 2. correct 3. correct
4. convenient 5. inventory

Lesson 31

A. 1. paste 2. treasure 3. blouse

B. 1. [hīr] 2. [ro͞o′ l r] 3. [hwēt]
4. [sprout]

Review: Unit 7

A. 1. b 2. a 3. c
4. d 5. b 6. d
7. a 8. b 9. c
10. d

B. 1. leader 2. disperse 3. impure
4. surrender 5. subservient

Test: Unit 7

A. 1. d 2. c 3. a 4. c
5. a 6. b 7. d 8. c
9. a 10. d

B. 1. c 2. a 3. d 4. a
5. b

C. 1. b 2. c 3. a 4. d
5. c

Unit 8

Lesson 32

A. Sample synonyms and dictionary definitions are provided.
1. Synonyms include adversary, opponent. antagonist: one that contends with, opposes, or resists.
2. Synonyms include sophisticated. cosmopolitan: having wide international sophistication.
3. Synonyms include distressing. disquieting: disturbing, alarming.
4. Synonyms include to infringe. encroach: to advance beyond the usual or proper limits.
5. Synonyms include venturous. enterprising: marked by an independent energetic spirit and by readiness to undertake or experiment.
6. Synonyms include outing. excursion: expedition, pleasure trip, digression.
7. Synonyms include to salute. hail: precipitation in the form of small balls or lumps of ice; to greet, call to attract attention.
8. Synonyms include fresh. novel: new and not resembling something formerly known or used; an invented prose narrative that is usually long and complex and deals especially with human experience.
9. Synonyms include unusual. outlandish: strikingly out of the ordinary, bizarre.
10. Synonyms include dread. trepidation: apprehension, agitation.

B. 1. 1; hail 2. 7; hail 3. 2; novel
4. 1; novel 5. 2; hail

C. 1. antagonist 2. cosmopolitan
3. excursion 4. outlandish

D. Student drawings should include captions that use the vocabulary words.

Lesson 33

A. Sample synonyms and dictionary definitions are provided.
1. Synonyms include expression. aspect: a particular appearance of countenance, mien, a particular status that may be studied.
2. Synonyms include wary. circumspect: careful to consider all circumstances and possible consequences, prudent.
3. Synonyms include striking. conspicuous: obvious to the mind or eye.
4. Synonyms include detestable. despicable: deserving to be despised.
5. Synonyms include outlook. prospect: possibility; to explore an area, especially for minerals.
6. Synonyms include to indicate. specify: to name or state explicitly or in detail.
7. Synonyms include example. specimen: an individual, item, or part considered typical of a group, class, or whole.
8. Synonyms include ghost. specter: something that haunts or perturbs the mind.
9. Synonyms include to theorize. speculate: to reflect, to be curious or doubtful about, to take a business risk.
10. Synonyms include mistrust. suspect: doubtful, questionable; one who is suspected; to have doubts of, distrust.

B. 1. 5; prospect 2. 4; suspect 3. 2; prospect
4. 1; suspect 5. 3; prospect

C. 1. specify 2. conspicuous 3. speculate
4. specimen 5. specter

Lesson 34

A. Sample synonyms and dictionary definitions are provided.
1. Synonyms include habitual. chronic: marked by long duration or frequent recurrence.
2. Synonyms include account. chronicle: a usually continuous historical account; to list, describe.
3. Synonyms include in time order. chronological: arranged according to the order of time.
4. Synonyms include simultaneous. contemporary: happening, existing, living, or coming into being during the same period of time; one of the same or nearly the same age as another.
5. Synonyms include to coordinate. synchronize: to happen at the same time.
6. Synonyms include to moderate. temper: to dilute or qualify; calmness of mind, composure.
7. Synonyms include moody. temperamental: marked by excessive sensitivity and impulsive changes of mood.
8. Synonyms include forbearance. temperance: moderation in action, thought, or feeling.
9. Synonyms include tumult. tempest: a violent storm, an uproar.
10. Synonyms include rhythm. tempo: rate of motion or activity, pace.

B. 1. 4; contemporary 2. 1; chronic 3. 3; chronic
4. 2; temperance 5. 3; contemporary

C. 1. correct 2. tempo 3. chronological
4. correct 5. tempest

Lesson 35

Student words will vary; sample dictionary definitions are provided.
1. break: to separate into parts with sudden violence
2. able: having sufficient resources to accomplish something
3. rely: to be dependent
4. trust: assured reliance on the character of someone or something
5. class: a group, set, or kind sharing common attributes
6. mobile: capable of moving or being moved
7. handle: to act on or perform a required function
8. bear: to support or sustain
9. honest: reputable, respectable
10. taint: corrupt; spoil

Review: Unit 8

1. b 2. c 3. a 4. c
5. d 6. a 7. d 8. b
9. c 10. a

Test: Unit 8

A. 1. c 2. a 3. b 4. a
5. d 6. c 7. a 8. a
9. d 10. b

B. 1. a 2. c 3. b 4. c
5. c

C. 1. c 2. a 3. d 4. b
5. b